The Land and People of

BOLIVIA

PORTRAITS OF THE NATIONS SERIES

The Land and People of®
BOLIVIA

by David Nelson Blair

J. B. LIPPINCOTT   NEW YORK

Country maps by Robert Romagnoli

Every effort has been made to locate the copyright holders
of all copyrighted photographs and to secure the necessary
permission to reproduce them. In the event of any questions arising
as to their use, the publisher will be glad to make necessary
changes in future printings and editions.

THE LAND AND PEOPLE OF
is a registered trademark of
Harper & Row, Publishers, Inc.

Library of Congress Cataloging-in-Publication Data
Blair, David Nelson.
    The land and people of Bolivia / David Nelson Blair.
        p.   cm. — (Portraits of the nations series)
    Includes bibliographical references.
    Summary: Introduces the history, geography, people, culture,
government, and economy of Bolivia.
    ISBN 0-397-32382-4 : $. — ISBN 0-397-32383-2 (lib. bdg.) :
$
    1. Bolivia—Juvenile literature.   [1. Bolivia.]   I. Title.
II. Series.
F3308.5.B58 1990   89-39721
984—dc20   CIP
                                                                 AC

1   2   3   4   5   6   7   8   9   10
First Edition

For Jennifer Vargas

Acknowledgments

The author is grateful to the people who offered valuable help and encouragement during the preparation of this book. He also appreciates the earlier contribution of so many Bolivians who made him welcome in their country, some even opening their homes to him.

The author is especially indebted to Ann Alborta, Marc Aronson, Mary Blair, Raymond Blair, Maria Cantwell, the Crisanto Copa family, Charles Kozischek, Anthony Salamone, Sara Sarmiento, Anita Vargas, and Julie Vargas; also to Maria-Teresa Campero, Embassy of Bolivia, Washington, D.C.; Lisa Famolare, Conservation International; Farida Khan (Warwick, R.I.) and Jenny Murillo (La Paz), Foster Parents Plan; Alvin Cohen, Lehigh University; and Hans C. Buechler, Syracuse University.

Two libraries in Easton, Pennsylvania, provided valuable facilities and reference help: Easton Area Public Library and David Bishop Skillman Library at Lafayette College.

Errors or misinterpretations in this book are the responsibility of the author alone.

Contents

THE WORLD

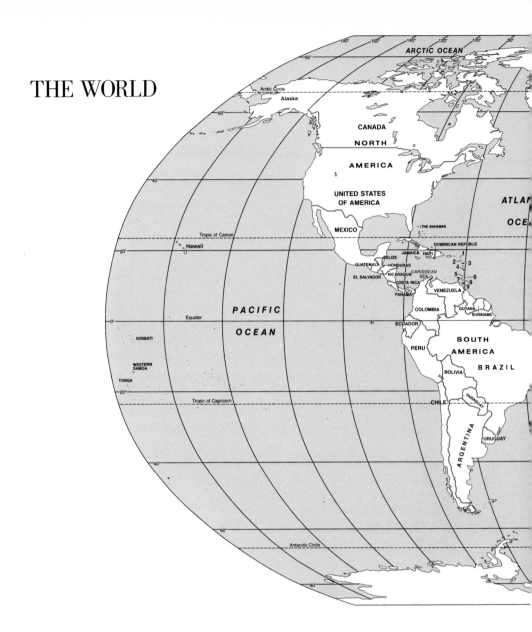

This world map is based on a projection developed by Arthur H. Robinson. The shape of each country and its size, relative to other countries, are more accurately expressed here than in previous maps. The map also gives equal importance to all of the continents, instead of placing North America at the center of the world. *Used by permission of the Foreign Policy Association.*

Legend

———— International boundaries

---------- Disputed or undefined boundaries

Projection: Robinson

| 0 | 1000 | 2000 | 3000 Miles |

| 0 | 1000 | 2000 | 3000 Kilometers |

Caribbean Nations

1. Anguilla
2. St. Christopher and Nevis
3. Antigua and Barbuda
4. Dominica
5. St. Lucia
6. Barbados
7. St. Vincent
8. Grenada
9. Trinidad and Tobago

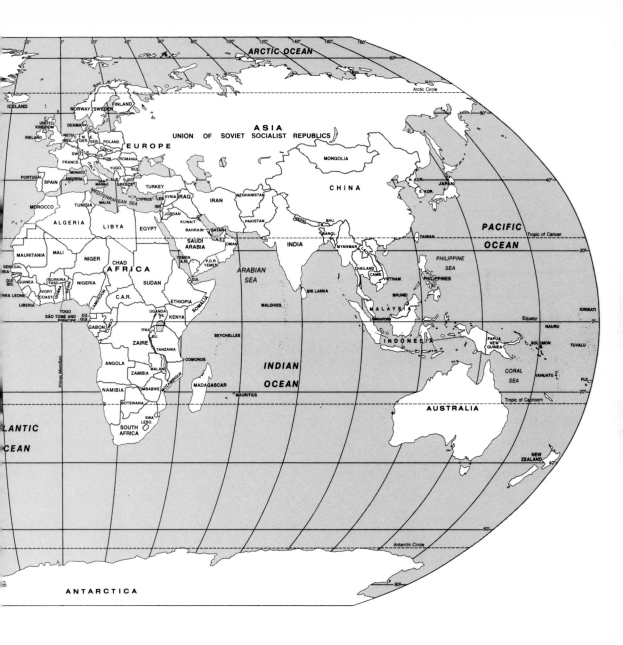

Abbreviations

ALB.	—Albania	C.A.R.	—Central African Republic	LEB.	—Lebanon	RWA.	—Rwanda
AUS.	—Austria	CZECH.	—Czechoslovakia	LESO.	—Lesotho	S. KOR.	—South Korea
BANGL.	—Bangladesh	DJI.	—Djibouti	LIE.	—Liechtenstein	SWA.	—Swaziland
BEL.	—Belgium	E.GER.	—East Germany	LUX.	—Luxemburg	SWITZ.	—Switzerland
BHU.	—Bhutan	EQ. GUI.	—Equatorial Guinea	NETH.	—Netherlands	U.A.E.	—United Arab Emirates
BU.	—Burundi	GUI. BIS.	—Guinea Bissau	N. KOR.	—North Korea	W. GER.	—West Germany
BUL.	—Bulgaria	HUN.	—Hungary	P.D.R.–YEMEN	—People's Democratic	YEMEN A.R.	—Yemen Arab Republic
CAMB.	—Cambodia	ISR.	—Israel		Republic of Yemen	YUGO.	—Yugoslavia

Mini Facts

OFFICIAL NAME: Republic of Bolivia *(República de Bolivia)*

LOCATION: landlocked in central South America with Brazil to the north and east, Paraguay to the southeast, Argentina to the south, and Chile and Peru to the west

AREA: 424,165 square miles (1,098,581 square kilometers)

CAPITAL: officially Sucre, but most government activities are based in La Paz

LARGEST CITIES: La Paz, Santa Cruz, Cochabamba, Oruro, Potosí, Sucre, Tarija

POPULATION: 7,400,000 (1990 estimate); 6,730,000 (1987)
Growth: 2.8 percent per year
Age Distribution: 43 percent under 15; 70 percent under 30
Sex Distribution: male 49.25 percent; female 50.75 percent

LIFE EXPECTANCY: male 48.6 years; female 53.0 years

INFANT MORTALITY: 12.4 percent

MAJOR LANGUAGES: Spanish, Quechua, Aymara

ADULT LITERACY: total 63.1 percent; male 75.8 percent; female 51.4 percent

RELIGION: Roman Catholicism, often combined with ancient American religions

UNIT OF CURRENCY: boliviano

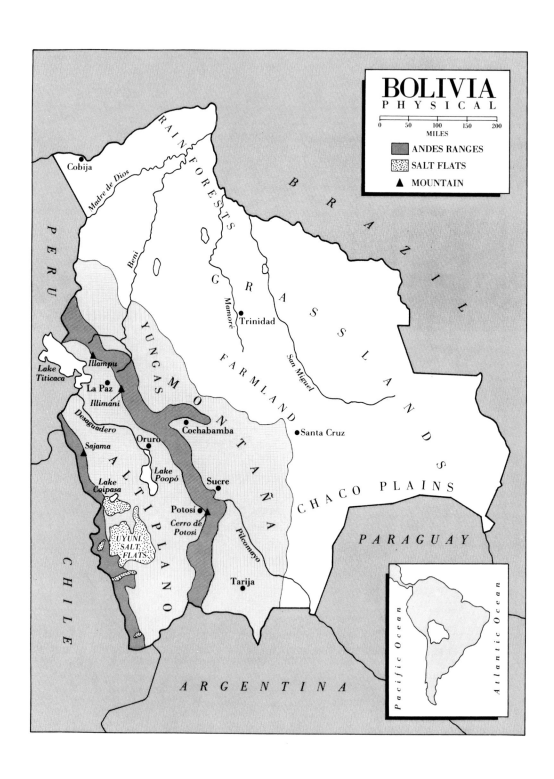

BOLIVIA
PHYSICAL

0   50   100   150   200
MILES

ANDES RANGES
SALT FLATS
▲ MOUNTAIN

Cobija

PERU

Madre de Dios

RAIN FORESTS

BRAZIL

Beni

GRASSLANDS

Mamoré

Trinidad

San Miguel

Lake
Titicaca

Illampu

La Paz ▲
Illimani

YUNGAS

FARMLAND

MONTAÑA

Desaguadero

Sajama ▲

Oruro

Cochabamba

Santa Cruz

ALTIPLANO

Lake
Poopó

Lake
Coipasa

Sucre

CHACO PLAINS

Potosi
Cerro de
Potosí

UYUNI
SALT
FLATS

Pilcomayo

PARAGUAY

Tarija

CHILE

ARGENTINA

Pacific Ocean

Atlantic Ocean

CHAPTER I

The *Diablada*

A commanding figure with helmet and sword has entered the crowded plaza. His shield bears the cross of the Roman Catholic Church. The kerchiefs hanging from his belt are red, yellow, and green, the colors of Bolivia. His huge blue eyes fix on the sinister figures dancing as the bands play their special devil marches. What an outrage! How can this be happening right in front of the cathedral dedicated to the Virgin? Saint Michael raises his sword and steps forward to tame the devils.

There is one dancer for each of the seven sins: pride, avarice, lust, anger, gluttony, envy, and sloth. Serpents spring from their foreheads. Twisted horns rise high. As the devils move, the sun glints on their huge eyes and pointed teeth. The hair from horse and ox tails and embroidered lizards, toads, and snakes decorate their robes. Jewels sparkle

· 1 ·

from their capes. But the saint is courageous. When his struggle with the devils is over, good has triumphed. Even Lucifer, the most elaborately costumed devil of all, has been shamed by Michael.

With their performance over and Lent just a few hours away, Saint Michael and the devils enter the church, remove their masks, and become mortal again. Then they hear Mass in honor of the Virgin of the Mineshaft.

The *diablada*, the devil dance, is the center of a festival that draws thousands of people every year to Oruro, Bolivia's fourth-largest city. It is no wonder that the Virgin of the Mineshaft is honored here. The rugged hills that loom nearby hold minerals that gave the city a reason for being four centuries ago. Success and failure in the mines has meant prosperity at times and poverty at others—for Oruro and Bolivia alike.

On the Saturday of Carnival, visitors and townspeople fill temporary bleachers along the main avenue. More line the streets or look on from windows, balconies, and walls. The activity will last from eight in the morning until nightfall.

The devils are the most famous of the dancing companies that appear that day, but there are dozens of others. One acts out the struggle between the Spanish and the Incas, a monumental clash in the history of South America. Another represents the black slaves who worked and mostly died in the mines of the old Spanish empire. Other companies represent the lowland cultures of Bolivia's east and the llama herders of the country's highlands. Dancers even portray wildlife. All join a grand parade that travels twenty blocks to the plaza. There they perform the precise, disciplined movements which they have practiced for months.

The devil dance itself is an old tradition. Various accounts, many of them mythical, explain its origins. One describes Spaniards of colonial

A masked devil dancer stands in front of the monument to miners in Oruro. United
Nations.

times who appeared as devils to frighten Indians into revealing the location of rich mines. Another tells of a miner who fell asleep in a shaft after making an offering to the devil. He awoke to find the devil dancing in front of him. The devil left the mine, still continuing his dance, and the man followed along in the first devil dance.

Historians trace the dance at least to the 1790's, but over the years it evolved and costumes became more and more elaborate. Saint Michael first appeared in 1818. At times there has also been a special devil dressed in white wool. Other dancers would seem to faint when he brushed against them. He represented the mine gas, the silent killer of thousands of miners over the centuries.

The carnival to which the dance belongs is a final release before the Catholic faithful observe the strict lifestyle required during Lent. Other Bolivian cities conduct similar festivals, as do other cities worldwide. The one in New Orleans, for example, is called Mardi Gras. In Rio de Janeiro, as in Oruro, it is known simply as Carnival. These festivals are very different in their details. Costumes, dances, and the figures portrayed vary widely, and they often include non-Christian features. In Mardi Gras the pagan figure King Neptune rules.

The Oruro festival has its *roots* in Catholic culture, yet here too there is something else—something old and deep. The crowd watching the Saturday dances supplies a few hints. Spectators may hear the name Supay, and no such figure appears in Catholic tradition. All around are Hispanic people, as one would expect to find in a South American country. But these are a minority. What seems Catholic is also Indian. Even before the Spanish came to the land, there were legends of the triumph over monsters. The defeat of the devils has its roots in these tales too. Saint Michael is a newcomer.

Indian tradition is even more visible in the days before the spectacle of carnival Saturday. On the Friday eight days earlier, a few dozen people meet near a stone serpent at the south edge of Oruro. They leave a *ch'alla*, an offering of liquor, cookies, or wool. The following Tuesday, *ch'allas* are offered in countless Oruro houses, the owners seeking to bring good fortune to their homes in the coming year. The next day a *ch'alla* is given again, this time at a stone image of a toad at the north edge of the city.

On Carnival Friday, the pace of activity increases, and miners play a special role. A *ch'alla* is offered to the stone image of a condor at the west edge of town. Later, offerings are made in the mines themselves. Before the 1960's (and occasionally later on) the miners sacrificed llamas in the mines. The act was a plea for safety to the devil of Catholic tradition. But the devil is also the hill spirit Supay remembered from a time before any Spaniard had breathed the thin air of the Andes.

Just as the devil dance has Hispanic and Indian roots, so do the people themselves. The Hispanic face appears more often to the rest of the world, but the Indian face is every bit as much a part of the nation. In the same way, Bolivia's industrial face has been the most visible to the outside through its mining. Yet miners are a minority in a land of farmers, herders, and market vendors. Finally, there is the land itself. Foreigners usually think of Bolivia as a highland nation, a land of llamas and tall mountains. Again the view is incomplete. Bolivia's vast, flat stretches of rain forests, grasslands, and dry plains reach into the heart of South America. Bolivia is a nation of distinct parts. To know these parts—what they are, how they affect one another, how they are blending and changing—is to know Bolivia.

CHAPTER II

More Than Just Mountains

Sometimes a thin layer of clouds hangs over the flat lowlands of eastern Bolivia. Through gaps in the clouds, air travelers leaving Santa Cruz can see the tropical land below, grayish green through the humid air and broken by winding, muddy rivers. After flying west for a while, they see the land rise. Eventually high hills poke through the cloud layer into the dryer, clearer air above, their peaks covered with lush forests. These would be mountains in most places, but in Bolivia they are foothills. The land continues to rise until it completely overtakes the cloud layer, and the two form a jagged, temporary coast between earth and sky.

As the jetliner nears La Paz still farther west, a towering mountain range reaches up toward the plane, then gives way to a bleak plateau. The pilot aims for the extra-long runway at the world's highest large

Geography in Brief

MAJOR REGIONS: two ranges of the Andes mountains; altiplano (a high plain between the ranges); montaña (foothills and valleys descending from the Andes); eastern lowlands

HIGHEST MOUNTAINS: Sajama, 21,391 feet (6,520 meters); Illimani, 21,201 (6,462 meters)

LOWEST PLAIN: southernmost borderland with Brazil, about 300 feet (90 meters)

LARGEST LAKES: Titicaca, shared with Peru, 3,500 square miles (9,100 square kilometers); Poopó, normally about 1,000 square miles (2,600 square kilometers), but area can more than double during rainy season

LONGEST RIVERS: Beni, Madre de Dios, and Mamoré (all major tributaries of Brazil's Amazon River)

MOST RAINFALL: northern rain forests, 98 inches (2,500 millimeters) per year

LEAST RAINFALL: southern altiplano, 10 inches (250 millimeters) per year

airport. The plane needs this added length because high-speed landings are necessary in thin air. When its tires touch the pavement, the air *is* thin because the runway is two and a half miles (four kilometers) above sea level.

The flight has lasted less than an hour, yet it has crossed the four distinct regions of Bolivia. Each has its own terrain, climate, wildlife, and resources. Within the nation's borders are tropical rain forests and arid salt flats. The Potosí and Pando areas are as different as the condors and crocodiles that occupy them.

Located in central South America, Bolivia forms a rough triangle about 800 miles (1,300 kilometers) on each side. Its modern boundaries leave it completely surrounded by five other nations: Brazil to the north and east, Paraguay to the southeast, Argentina to the south, Chile and Peru to the west. Bolivia has only the fifth-largest land area among the countries of South America and appears tiny next to giant Brazil. Yet it is about the size of Texas and California combined, covering 424,165 square miles (1,098,581 square kilometers). This area is divided into nine states called departments, the largest of which is nearly the size of Montana.

Bolivia falls entirely within the Earth's tropical belt, yet its highest peaks are permanently snow covered. Since temperatures drop with elevation (an average of 3°F per 1,000 feet of altitude), a high mountain can be snowcapped even if it is near the equator. More than any other characteristic, altitude sets apart the four distinct regions of Bolivia.

The Andean Ranges

At the top are Sajama, Illimani, and three other Bolivian peaks that are all higher than any mountain in North America. They are part of the vast Andes mountain chain that runs the length of western South America and breaks into two separate ranges that pass through Bolivia. The narrow western range forms a natural boundry between Chile and

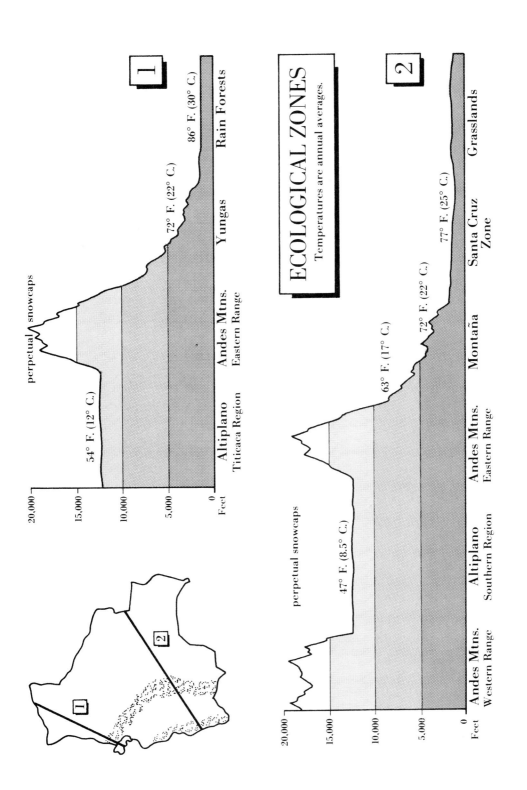

ECOLOGICAL ZONES
Temperatures are annual averages.

1

perpetual snowcaps

54° F. (12° C.)

72° F. (22° C.)

86° F. (30° C.)

Altiplano
Titicaca Region

Andes Mtns.
Eastern Range

Yungas

Rain Forests

20,000

15,000

10,000

5,000

0

Feet

2

perpetual snowcaps

47° F. (8.5° C.)

63° F. (17° C.)

72° F. (22° C.)

77° F. (25° C.)

Andes Mtns.
Western Range

Altiplano
Southern Region

Andes Mtns.
Eastern Range

Montaña

Santa Cruz
Zone

Grasslands

20,000

15,000

10,000

5,000

0

Feet

Bolivia. Here Sajama's summit stands 21,391 feet (6,520 meters) above sea level.

The other range extends southeast from Peru to a point just east of the city of Potosí, then south to the Argentine border. Illimani is the highest in this range, reaching 21,201 feet (6,462 meters) above sea level. It is Bolivia's most familiar mountain because it towers above La Paz, the nation's largest city. Usually its triple peak dominates the view from the city below, though sometimes it is lost in a still mist that can linger even when the rest of the sky is clear.

The Illimani's triple peak dwarfs La Paz.   Doranne Jacobson

Only a few tough animal species can survive in these ranges, where after sundown the temperature plummets because the thin, dry air loses its heat quickly. Giant condors fly as high as 20,000 feet (6,000 meters) and lay their eggs between a few sticks on inaccessible rock ledges. Wool-bearing animals related to the camel are native to the ranges, and sheep have also survived there since they were brought from Europe centuries ago. The vicuña, the smallest of the camellike animals, has light, soft wool. Many are wild, grazing on scarce clumps of mountain grass, but others are herded by people, as are their cousins the llamas and alpacas. A few rodents, such as the silver-gray chinchillas, can also survive in the mountains, but for the most part insects cannot.

Abundant minerals have drawn people to the mountains. In the eastern range silver and tin have been mined in great quantities. There are also deposits of lead, bismuth, zinc, antimony, gold, and wolfram. The western range is not as rich, though there are significant deposits of nitrites and copper within its slopes. Human settlement in the mountains has never been great, however. Except for those in mining camps and tiny villages, Bolivian highlanders prefer to live on a broad, high plateau between the two mountain ranges.

The Altiplano

The Spanish word *altiplano* means "high plain" and well describes the table of land that stretches 500 miles (800 kilometers) from Peru to Argentina at an average altitude of 13,000 feet (4,000 meters). Two thirds of this plateau, the largest in the Andes, falls within Bolivia. As in the mountains, conditions are hard. Unpredictable hail is a danger, and nights during any month of the year may bring frost. This dry, almost treeless region is covered by windy grasslands and desert. As in the mountains, only a few insects can stand the altitude. Herds of grazing animals feed on mountain grass that shoots up in coarse clumps. Small predators such as the fox feed on small domestic animals and wild rodents. Among these rodents is the long-eared, long-legged mara. Another is the viscacha, which often suns itself on rocks and whistles a warning if humans pass by.

Life for both people and animals in the northern altiplano is more comfortable because of a huge lake on the border with Peru. Lake Titicaca is the highest large lake in the world and is so deep (1,235 feet—376 meters) that early people believed it was bottomless. Totora reeds grow near the lakeshore and are used to make everything from mats to furniture to fishing boats. Fishing has been especially good since trout was introduced to the lake earlier in the century. Huge frogs and an abundance of bird species—gulls, ducks, and geese—also make it their home.

The lake's 3,500 square miles (9,100 square kilometers) allow plenty of evaporation, making the air nearby relatively moist. Rainfall averages 26 inches (650 millimeters) per year. Water holds heat well, so the lake also keeps the immediate area warmer than the rest of the altiplano. The slopes leading to the shore have been terraced for farming, and potatoes, barley, alfalfa, quinoa (a high-protein native grain), peas, broadbeans, and onions all grow. Domesticated animals have been introduced to the region. Some donkeys and horses get by, though the altitude is tough on them. Hogs, chickens, rabbits, and guinea pigs are used for meat. Some cattle live here, but more common are herds of sheep and the native llamas and alpacas.

The only disadvantage of the lake is the danger of flooding. Crops and livestock can be lost during years of unusually heavy rainfall.

Farther south, the altiplano is cooler and drier still, receiving only about 14 inches (350 millimeters) of rain per year. The soil is a bit salty, and there is less water for irrigation. Nonetheless llama and alpaca herds still graze here on the increasingly thin mountain grass, and enough barley and quinoa is grown to feed the local sheep.

In the southernmost part of the altiplano, the conditions get tougher. It is colder yet, and rainfall is only about 10 inches (250 millimeters) per year. A few llama and alpaca herds survive here, but the crops from the salty soil are just enough to keep them alive. The region is especially prone to killing frost, and the dry season, April to January, is two months longer than in the rest of the altiplano.

The salt lakes here are nothing like freshwater Titicaca. Poopó is large but shallow, never deeper than fifteen feet (four and a half meters) when the water is at normal levels. This unusual lake expands greatly when there is extraordinary rainfall. Normally its northern shore is dozens of miles south of Oruro. At times, however, it fills a narrow depression to form a branch that almost reaches the city's southern edge. Poopó and a smaller lake, Coipasa, do not support the wildlife that Titicaca does. Thousands of years ago, other salt lakes existed in the area, but they have dried up, leaving arid salt flats in the southwestern altiplano. The largest, the Uyuni flat, covers 3,500 square miles (9,100 square kilometers), larger than Delaware and Rhode Island combined. These lands are almost completely barren.

The little rain that falls in the altiplano gathers in streams that never reach an ocean. These run into the lakes or into the Desaguadero River, which flows from Titicaca to Poopó. The water remains in the lakes until it evaporates back into the dry air. These high-altitude waters are beautifully clear, and tiny pebbles and sand grains are visible at the bottoms of shallow steams.

Despite the extreme altitude, the altiplano is the most densely popu-lated region of Bolivia. Because the soils tend to be better near the eastern mountain range, and because minerals are most abundant in that range, people have settled the eastern altiplano most heavily. Three major cities have grown up near the eastern range (while no important centers are located along the western range). Oruro and Potosí are principally mining communities on the central altiplano.

The third, La Paz, stands to the north near Lake Titicaca. It fills a canyon cut into the altiplano right at the edge of the eastern range. During brief rainshowers, the streets descending the canyon slopes literally become shallow rapids. This water will eventually reach an ocean, but not the Pacific a couple hundred miles away. Instead it will wind for thousands of miles along a northeasterly course that will take it to the Amazon River in Brazil and finally to the Atlantic. But first it must travel through the lower regions of Bolivia.

The Montaña

Roads from La Paz cut through the broken eastern range just as rivers do. They wind through countless hairpin turns along steep cliffs. Some are just narrow trails that are so treacherous that traffic is allowed in only one direction at a time. Just fifty miles from La Paz, the road has descended 7,000 feet (2,100 meters). Gone are the thin grasses and dry air of the high plain. Instead, the air is moist, and steep slopes are thick with rich, green vegetation.

This is the montaña, popularly called the "eyebrow of the mountain." It is a wide band of foothills and valleys along the eastern slope of the Andes. It is a controversial region because cocaine is refined from the leaves of the coca shrub that grows here. For centuries, coca leaves have been chewed raw or brewed as tea. In the 1970's and 1980's, however, cultivation increased greatly to supply cocaine traffickers. (Chapter 13 discusses cocaine and what it has meant to Bolivia.)

A road winds through steep hills and valleys in the yungas.   Doranne Jacobson

Even within the montaña, the climate varies considerably with the changing altitude. Most of the region is between 3,900 and 8,500 feet (1,200 to 2,600 meters) above sea level. It is cool or temperate in the higher areas and subtropical or even tropical farther down. Average rainfall can vary from 17 to 47 inches per year (430 to 1,200 millimeters).

The climate allows for at least one good growing season each year. The higher valleys are green with pepper trees and pacae—shade trees that are used to protect coffee plants. Since frost occurs only in the highest spots, potatoes and barley enjoy better growing seasons than on the altiplano; and corn, wheat, and grapes also grow. Dairy cattle, poultry, pigs, and goats produce milk and meat here.

Three major cities are located among the higher valleys and hills: Tarija, Bolivia's southernmost major city; Sucre, the historical capital; and Cochabamba, the third-largest city. Many consider Cochabamba to have an ideal climate year-round. It is near the equator, so there is little temperature difference between summer and winter. Yet it is high enough (8,000 feet—2,400 meters) to escape the intense heat that plagues most of the Earth's tropical zone. At the same time, it is low enough to avoid the constant frosts and other disadvantages of high altitude.

The lower parts of the montaña are rich with forests of green pine, black walnut, laurel, and cedar. No dry months interrupt a year-round growing season that can produce coca, coffee, tobacco, sugarcane, grapes, sweet potatoes, and peanuts. Figs, peaches, citrus fruits, pineapples, and bananas also prosper. Northern areas in the lower montaña are called the *yungas*. This is the name once used by ancient highland civilizations for the lands where they established colonies. Though the *yungas* are not much different from the rest of the lower montaña, Bolivians still think of them as a distinct region.

Montaña wildlife is also more varied than in the mountains or altiplano. Jaguars, the largest of South American cats, hunt through the lower regions looking for deer. Armadillos, opossums, and huge vicious weasels called tayras also live here. Insect life increases the lower one gets. These lower regions are not densely populated and contain no major cities. Still, a significant number of people are found on plantations and in smaller communities.

The Eastern Lowlands

The regions discussed so far lie in bands that account for less than half of Bolivia's land. By contrast, the lowlands spread out for hundreds of miles to the northeast. This land, mostly 300 to 1,500 feet (90 to 450 meters) above sea level, is part of the vast South American interior that has never been thoroughly explored, let alone settled. In the last half century people have begun to tap oil and natural gas reserves, but incredible timber resources—more than a hundred types of commercially usable wood—remain largely untouched. Transportation difficulties account for this. To reach markets, products have to be moved over mountains or across thousands of miles of wilderness. On the other hand, the isolation has helped prevent the destruction of ecologically important forests. A new conservation program now protects some of this land.

Wildlife in this region is still more abundant and varied than in the valleys and foothills. Jaguars hunt over wide areas of jungles and grasslands for deer, wild pigs, and giant rodents called capybaras that slip into lakes and rivers to escape. As is typical in tropical areas, the insect species can barely be counted. Mosquitoes, flies, ants, termites, and gnats are the most troublesome to humans.

The northernmost area is covered by Amazon rain forests and is the

Capybaras, the world's largest rodents, can each weigh over 100 pounds (45 kilograms).
Conservation International

hottest and wettest region of the nation, averaging about 98 inches (2,500 millimeters) of rain each year. Sloths, spider monkeys, and ocelots live here, along with a variety of birds, from vultures to brightly colored parakeets and toucans. Alligators hiding among thick weeds are often detectable only at night—when their eyes glow red in flashlight beams.

An ocelot hunts in dense forests.   Conservation International

Few people live in the region, though nomadic Indians survive here, and jungle products have attracted some settlers from the outside. Rubber comes from a few cultivated groves, but mostly from wild trees. Brazil nuts and snakeskins are also gathered from the wild. Still, there are no cities in the rain forests. Even Cobija, capital of the Pando department, is only a small town.

Just south of the forests, though still in northern Bolivia, vast ranges of grass and shrubs cover a region used for cattle ranching. A dry season runs from May to August, but enough rain falls at other times to cause flooding and to threaten livestock. Temperatures and rainfall vary a great deal within this region, but it is still one of the hottest and wettest places in Bolivia. There are many more people than in the rain forests, and Trinidad, Beni's capital, is a small city.

Farther south and completely within Santa Cruz department is a smaller zone of forests and rich land. This includes the city of Santa Cruz and lands to the northeast and is the most populated zone of the eastern lowlands. Santa Cruz, which recently became Bolivia's second largest city, is a frontier community that is expanding away from its central plaza along a series of concentric beltways. The zone around it has become the agricultural center of the nation, producing beef, poultry, cotton, sugarcane, corn, and rice. Rainfall averages 45 inches (1,150 millimeters) per year. Though residents are bothered by tropical insects, their gardens also attract large, brightly colored butterflies.

The rivers of the rain forests, the grasslands, and the Santa Cruz farmlands all flow to the northeast, eventually joining the Amazon River in Brazil. The Beni, Madre de Dios, and Mamoré are the largest. The banks and shallow, slow waters are home to crocodiles, water boas, salamanders, frogs, toads, cicadas, and billions of mosquitoes. Explor-

Papaya trees grow in warm, lowland Santa Cruz.   David Nelson Blair

ers have pulled vicious piranhas from the water without using hooks—just bits of meat tied to the ends of string.

The southernmost region of the Bolivian lowlands is the *chaco,* an expanse of dry, sandy plains and scrub forests. Thirty inches (750 millimeters) of rain fall each year on average, but it is unevenly distributed. That, along with a dry season that runs from April to November, leaves the region much more barren than the lowlands to the north. A large viper called the fer-de-lance and other snakes make their homes here, along with the usual tropical insects. Rheas, which run across the flat land like their cousin the ostrich, and storks live here as well. What rain does fall collects in streams that flow to the southeast, joining the Pilcomayo and Paraguay rivers and eventually reaching the Atlantic Ocean through the La Plata estuary between Argentina and Uruguay. Some cattle ranching takes place in the chaco, and there is considerable interest in its oil and gas reserves, but there are no cities in the region and it is so far only sparsely populated.

The ranges, the altiplano, the montaña, and the lowlands became Bolivia in 1825. The new nation was a mix not just of different regions but of different people. Bolivians are descended from ancestors who were once widely separated and who were as different from one another as the chaco is from the *yungas.*

Tiahuanaco, Kingdoms, and Kollasuyo

Bolivia's radically different regions were home to an amazing variety of ancient people. Migrants from North and Central America entered South America at least twenty thousand years ago and gradually settled the entire continent. Some created great highland civilizations that endured for centuries, only to disappear before the time of recorded history. Others spread across the lowlands, quickly losing touch with their past and their neighbors. For centuries, hundreds of distinct cultures survived in isolation across the vast continent.

Ancient peoples in what is now Bolivia had no common trait to suggest that their lands would someday be a nation. At the beginning of recorded history in South America, two conquests brought some of them under a single authority. But this did not make them citizens of a nation. Instead they spent three and a half centuries as subject peoples in two great empires—the first ruled from Cuzco, the second from Madrid.

The Isolated East

The lives and beliefs of ancient cultures east of the Andes varied with the terrain, climate, and creatures they encountered. The Mojo knew a world of water and dangerous cats. Long before written history in South America, they settled the damp Beni plains. Floods there lasted up to four months each year. They built raised platforms covered with soil so that their cooking fires were safe even when their homes were flooded. In drier seasons, the jaguar came and inspired them with its ferocity. The Mojo gave special status to any man wounded by one of the big cats.

The Yucare peoples of the montaña also revered the jaguar. In their legends, the dark patches visible on the moon became the eyes of a supernatural cat. To the east, the Chiriguano people similarly gave a place in the sky to the creature most familiar to them: The stars of the Southern Cross marked the head of the fleet-footed rhea, and the Milky Way became its road.

While variety was great among the ancient lowlanders, numbers were always small. Ultimately, the scattered cultures made little impression on modern Bolivia. Among the native South Americans, the Andes dwellers to the west were the most important to the nation that was to come.

The Legacy of the Highlanders

Ancient highland people had to learn how to survive in the harsh conditions of the altiplano and mountain ranges miles above sea level.

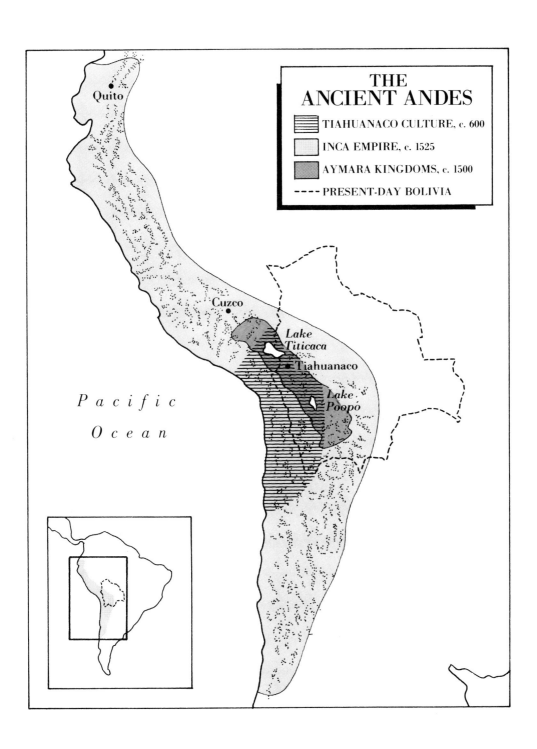

THE ANCIENT ANDES

- ▤ TIAHUANACO CULTURE, c. 600
- ▢ INCA EMPIRE, c. 1525
- ▨ AYMARA KINGDOMS, c. 1500
- - - - PRESENT-DAY BOLIVIA

Quito

Cuzco

Lake Titicaca

Tiahuanaco

Lake Poopó

Pacific Ocean

Before permanent communities developed, they hunted small game and discovered how to turn Lake Titicaca's totora reeds into fishing boats. They found that *yareta*, a root that grows on the altiplano, could be dried and used to feed fires.

Early people around Lake Titicaca learned to build reed boats like these. Hutchison Library/Brian Moser

In many other parts of the world, early peoples learned to grow crops before they thought to raise herds of animals. But agriculture was especially difficult in a land of year-round frost. So around 7000 B.C., before they planted seeds, the Andes dwellers learned to use the llamas and alpacas that shared their highlands. Wool from these animals could be woven into cords, ropes, or—most important—warm clothing to stave off the cold of the Andean night. Their droppings could be left to dry and then be used as fuel for cooking fires where wood was scarce.

Over the centuries, the herders learned new things. Animal droppings could also fertilize the crops, which the highlanders finally began to grow around 2500 B.C. Llamas and alpacas could also carry heavy loads. The animals became so valuable that they usually were not killed for food. Yet when they died naturally, they provided meat and hides as well as bones that could be carved into weaving tools. By 1000 B.C. llamas and alpacas were fully domesticated. They had played an important role in human survival, and the local men and women had established a bond with these animals that continues in Bolivia today.

The highlanders were less likely to wander once they began growing crops, and small villages formed as agriculture became commonplace. Gradually, farming techniques improved. Around Lake Titicaca early farmers dug canals and used the dirt they removed to build raised lanes, some the length of football fields. When the canals were flooded, crops on the raised ground could be easily watered. The water in the canals would also collect heat in the daytime and gradually release it at night, protecting the crops from frost. (The technique has impressed archeologists, who believe it might be useful today in places where advanced farm machinery is not available.)

With their survival fairly secure, trade and conquest spread the influence of some villages. Around 1200 B.C. the Chavín of Peru were the first to influence a large area of the Andes. They were impressed

A Stone City

Long before the Incas, ancient fisherman took reed boats onto Lake Titicaca to bring in the catch. To the southeast, farmers toiled over some 200,000 acres (80,000 hectares) of potatoes and other crops. The labor had a purpose: A hungry city stood at the center of the farm district. Fourteen centuries ago, there were many mouths to feed in Tiahuanaco—perhaps 20,000, perhaps 40,000. This was a center of trade for a region that stretched from the Pacific Coast to the montaña.

But it was more. One prominent carved gateway twice the height of a person was decorated with scores of figures. All faced a larger figure with a fan-shaped headdress and decorated staffs. This Staff God had catlike features, and it is possible that he was inspired by memories of the Chavín culture, which centuries earlier had worshiped pumas. The spread of Staff God's image on pottery suggests that Tiahuanaco was an early center of religion.

The city itself covered at least 2,600 acres (1,000 hectares). Most of the buildings were modest adobe structures, but the city center was grand. Across the 125-acre (50-hectare) site ran two wide avenues lined with massive buildings—perhaps temples and residences of the city's upper class. Among them were Staff God's gateway and pillarlike carved figures standing three or four times the height of a person. Nearby walls covered with carved faces enclosed a sunken courtyard. The gateway, figures, faces, monuments, and blocks were all formed from stone. Builders had shaped blocks as heavy as 100 tons (90 metric tons), and fit them together so perfectly that they required no mortar.

The stonemasons of Tiahuanaco were masters. They and their people vanished long ago, but their showcase of stone architecture survives today on the Bolivian altiplano.

A stone entryway at Tiahuanaco.   David Nelson Blair

Stone faces line a sunken court.   David Nelson Blair

by the pumas that roamed their territories, and feline deities decorate the pottery they left behind.

Around 400 B.C., the important Tiahuanaco culture began on the altiplano south of Lake Titicaca. Its people developed their own style of pottery, learned to work with stone and metal, and harvested their crops despite the climate. Their most inspiring accomplishment was the city they built 13 miles (21 kilometers) southeast of the lake.

Also called Tiahuanaco, it became the center of widespread trade. Between A.D. 375 and 1000, its people traveled across the highlands

A well-preserved stone face. David Nelson Blair

The Staff God on the Gateway to the Sun.   David Nelson Blair

into what is now southern Peru, along the Pacific coast into what is now Chile, and to the east into the montaña. Throughout this area, archeologists have found their pottery, some of it recognizable because it is decorated with Tiahuanaco's Staff God. Trade in the east was especially important because it brought in coca leaves and other products that did not grow on the altiplano. Thus all regions of Bolivia except the low-lands were unified in these ancient times.

The Tiahuanaco culture reached its peak in the century or two after A.D. 600, but then slowly declined for reasons no one today knows. It finally disappeared around 1200. Over the next two centuries a new series of kingdoms grew around Lake Titicaca and spread to the south throughout the Bolivian altiplano. These had names such as Kollas, Lupacas, and Charcas. Soon their people developed fortified towns and placed communities on hilltops, as well as along the lakeshore. They refined the ancient herding practices and maintained trading colonies in the montaña. But these kingdoms did not form a united society. There was, however, a common bond—language. The highlanders all spoke Aymara, one of three major languages used in Bolivia today.

The First Conquest

The second major language, Quechua, began as a foreign language. Early in the fifteenth century, it arrived with an army.

The Aymara kingdoms had been fighting among themselves, and Kollas and Lupacas each tried to become the strongest of the Aymara realms. Both sought help from a nearby Quechua-speaking leader named Viracocha. Soon a Quechua army arrived and formed an alliance with Lupacas, and the time of independent Aymara kingdoms neared its end.

Viracocha was an Inca, a member of the royal family that ruled the Quechua people. (Strictly speaking, only a member of the Quechua royalty should be called an Inca.) For more than two hundred years the Inca dynasty had ruled a relatively small area northwest of the Aymara kingdoms. From his capital at Cuzco, Viracocha began conquering new territories. He told his new subjects that he was descended from a man placed in the world by the sun itself. His might seemed to prove that point. His son completely controlled Kollas and Lupacas by the 1460's. Over the next thirty years, Viracocha's grandson, Tupa Inca, became one of the greatest conquerors in world history. He expanded the Inca empire north past Quito to what is now the northern border of Ecuador, as well as south along the Pacific coast to the Maule River in what is now central Chile. All of the highland region around Lake Titicaca and far to the south fell under Inca control. These new lords called it Kollasuyo. Over the years there were Aymara rebellions against the invaders, but the Aymara were never united enough to expel them.

An Ancient Land with a Short History

Historians know little about South America before A.D. 1200 because no native culture invented writing. The Incas kept track of numbers with their *quipus*. But these knotted strings are like figures written in ledger books without titles or headings. They reveal nothing without the Inca accountants who knew what each knot stood for. Likewise, Inca history depended entirely on memory.

From the Incas, Spanish chroniclers learned the names and deeds of ten generations of Inca lords before Huayna Capac. Before that, the Incas told them, the world lived in darkness. They showed the Spaniards the ancient stone gateway at Tiahuanaco. But Staff God's gateway became the Gateway to the Sun—not because of its builders' intentions, but because the sun was an important *Inca*

The Incas bragged they would drink from the skulls of all who opposed them. Yet they had no wish to destroy those who would accept their rule. Tupa Inca ordered his troops not to pillage the new territories, and he dressed according to local customs when he visited conquered areas. The Aymara kept their language and their outposts in the montaña.

What the Incas did want was to rule. They sent administrators to oversee Aymara leaders. They sent *tucuyricos*, inspectors whose title meant "one who sees all." They succeeded in establishing a strong, centralized empire.

diety. They told the Spaniards that the nearby figures had been turned to stone by the sun. Once, they added, these had been giants who walked the world in the time of darkness.

In fact, darkness covered not the world, but Inca memory. Modern historians know that the earliest men and women of the Andes lived side by side with llamas and alpacas because archeologists have found weaving tools made from animal bones. They know how far a culture's traders traveled by recording where its pottery has been found. They can even estimate Tiahuanaco's population from the amount of ancient trash found around the city.

But without written records, historians can only guess what first drove some ancient family into the harsh Andes. No one today knows the names of the rulers of the Chavín and Tiahuanaco cultures. No one can repeat the stories that must have been told about Staff God. And historians can only guess why the enduring civilization at Tiahuanaco finally died out.

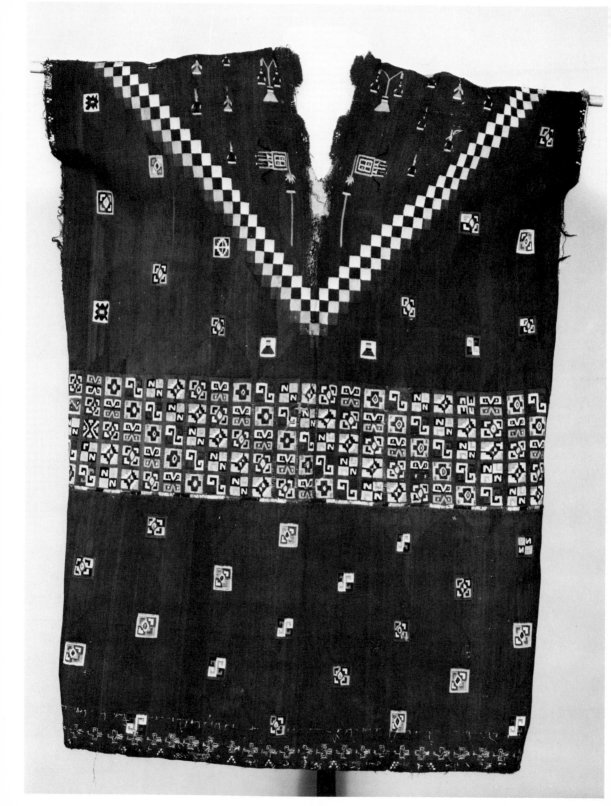

Large areas, including some along the Bolivian shore of Lake Titicaca, were terraced for farming. Roads, bridges, temples, palaces, aqueducts, baths, fountains, and new tools were introduced throughout the empire. The Inca system of record keeping was introduced; bunches of knotted strings called *quipus* kept track of births, deaths, and food stores. The Incas introduced a greater variety of food, ceramics, and metal objects. They built warehouses and distributed food and goods throughout their empire. Their system provided for orphans and the aged, and in times of famine, their food reserves helped their subjects to survive.

Naturally the Incas wanted something in return. They never invented currency, so they did not impose anything that resembled modern taxes. They did take land. In each conquered province, land was divided three ways: one part each for the sun, the ruler, and the people. The land for the people was not generous, only enough to ensure their survival. They may, though, have had access to the produce from the fields of the sun in times of crisis.

Even more important, the Incas demanded labor. In addition to working their own land, conquered people toiled on the lands of the sun and the ruler, supporting the Inca elite and filling their warehouses. Inca construction projects and the demand for servants meant more endless hours of hard work.

The Inca system brought compulsory labor into the lives of Aymara-speaking people of the altiplano region. They and their Quechua-speaking neighbors would live with that burden for four and a half centuries beyond the time of Tupa Inca.

By the mid-1520's, the Inca Empire stretched 2,500 miles (4,000

An Inca poncho. Neg. no. 332148, Department of Library Services, American Museum of Natural History

kilometers) along the Pacific coast of South America and took in roughly 6 million people. Tupa Inca's son Huayna Capac believed his empire covered nearly the entire world. As he saw it, Kollasuyo and the three other regions he controlled made up the Four Corners of the World. His capital was at the center of that world. In 1525, Huayna Capac had no reason to doubt that his was the most advanced and powerful civilization on Earth. He died that year without ever knowing that a pope in an unheard-of land had given away the Four Corners of the World.

CHAPTER IV

C H A P T E R   I V

New Lords in Upper Peru

In 1493 Pope Alexander VI divided the pagan territories of the world between two Christian monarchs. He decreed that a line ran from the North Pole, passed west of Europe, and continued to the South Pole. He gave King João II of Portugal the duty to spread Christianity east of the line, and he assigned Queen Isabella of Spain to do the same to the west.

And why not? The year before, the last Moslem territories in Spain had been conquered by Christian forces. At almost the same time, Alexander learned that Columbus had discovered lands far to the west. These two events surely signaled that Christianity was destined to spread farther. Alexander took steps to make it happen.

The Spanish and Portuguese rulers and their successors welcomed

Before Bolivia

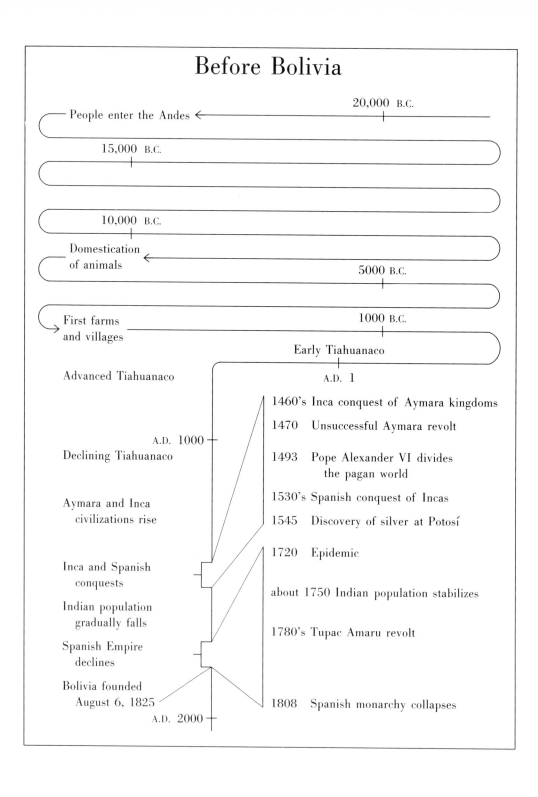

People enter the Andes ← 20,000 B.C.

15,000 B.C.

10,000 B.C.

Domestication of animals ←

5000 B.C.

First farms and villages

1000 B.C.

Early Tiahuanaco

Advanced Tiahuanaco

A.D. 1

1460's Inca conquest of Aymara kingdoms

1470 Unsuccessful Aymara revolt

A.D. 1000

Declining Tiahuanaco

1493 Pope Alexander VI divides the pagan world

1530's Spanish conquest of Incas

Aymara and Inca civilizations rise

1545 Discovery of silver at Potosí

1720 Epidemic

Inca and Spanish conquests

about 1750 Indian population stabilizes

Indian population gradually falls

1780's Tupac Amaru revolt

Spanish Empire declines

Bolivia founded August 6, 1825

1808 Spanish monarchy collapses

A.D. 2000

the task. Spain, in particular, was a wealthy and powerful nation capable of launching oceangoing ships. But it had seen Portugal become the leader in exploration with voyages down the coast of Africa. Spain wanted to catch up, but its reasons went beyond prestige and a desire to spread the faith. Alexander's decree gave Spain the right to explore and trade on its side of the line. The Spanish took that to mean they could conquer and rule anything they found. Kollasuyo happened to fall on Spain's side of the pope's line.

The Second Conquest

More than a generation passed between Alexander's decree and the arrival of Spaniards in the Andes. First Spain established colonies in the Caribbean. Then Hernán Cortés led a few hundred Spanish *conquistadores* into Mexico, gained allies among the Tlaxcalan people, and defeated the wealthy and powerful Aztec nation. Later explorers crossed the narrow isthmus of Central America and set up bases on the Pacific coast.

From there, Francisco Pizarro sailed down the west coast of South America and learned about an empire ruled from a capital high in the mountains. He returned to Spain, taking with him llamas, fine wool fabrics, and vases of gold and silver. King Carlos I was impressed—especially with the gold and silver. Pizarro received the title Governor and Captain General of Peru, and he left Spain with the right to conquer the Incas.

In 1532 Pizarro led a force of 168 Europeans into the Andes. Waiting was an empire defended by at least 30,000 soldiers. It seems impossible that Pizarro succeeded in winning the empire, but the Spaniard had several things in his favor. The first was luck.

By pure chance, he arrived within a few months of an Inca civil war.

The People of Upper Peru

The Spanish and other Europeans used "Indian" to refer to anyone belonging to the native peoples of the Western Hemisphere. It didn't matter that the Aymara and Quechua groups used a different language. It didn't matter that these descendants of major highland civilizations had little in common with the lowland Mojo. All were Indians.

Columbus, thinking he was near the coast of India, had first given the name to people he encountered in the Caribbean. It is still used today, but it is important to remember that Bolivian Indians vary a great deal among themselves. And their dress, languages, and lifestyles are very different from those of North American Indians.

Sixteenth-century Europeans argued at length about Indians. How should they be treated? Who were they? *What* were they? Some said that they were not really people at all, but in 1537 Pope Paul III declared that this viewpoint was heresy. No important Spaniard questioned the humanity of Indians. Instead, statesmen, religious scholars, and lawyers in Spain raised questions that seemed to show they were genuinely concerned about the Indians. Many wondered if it had been correct to overthrow Indian leaders.

The arguments had little effect on Spaniards in America. Pope Alexander VI had clearly stated that the Europeans were responsible for spreading Christianity to the Indians. How could

From the defeated side, Pizarro easily found allies against Atahuallpa, the victorious ruler. He also had superior weapons—crossbows, steel

anyone oppose conquests that led to the salvation of Indian souls? But the Spaniards did not act like concerned guardians, and a Spanish American society developed that treated the Indians as inferiors. Within a generation of the conquest, this hierarchy became more complicated as new classes appeared. Here are the ones most important in Upper Peru, ranked from highest to lowest in social standing:

—**Spaniards** were people born in Spain.

—**Creoles** were people born in the Americas who were descended from Europeans only.

—**Mestizas** (females) and **mestizos** (males or mixed groups) were descended from both Europeans and Indians. These terms were used throughout Spanish America, but in Upper Peru they usually referred to people who spoke, dressed, and acted more like Spaniards than Indians.

—**Cholas** (females) and **cholos** (males or mixed groups) also had both Spanish and Indian blood. These terms were used only in Upper Peru, usually for people who spoke, dressed, and acted more like Indians than Spaniards.

—**Indians** in Upper Peru were mostly the Aymara- and Quechua-speaking peoples who had once been subjects of the Inca Empire. However, the term was also applied to very different peoples, most of them in the lowlands.

swords, horses, and firearms including cannons. Some Inca soldiers thought that man, horse, sword, and gun were all parts of one terrifying creature. Finally, the Spanish leader knew that Cortés had succeeded against similar odds by capturing the Aztecs' ruler. Following that strategy, the Spaniards seized Atahuallpa and imprisoned him. The Inca's shocked subjects obeyed Pizarro's orders in hopes of winning their leader's release—which never came. Atahuallpa was eventually executed, and the Inca dynasty had lost its empire. The land destined to become Bolivia would first spend three hundred years as a colony of Spain.

Nonetheless, the Incas resisted for forty years. The Spanish crowned puppet Incas to rule at their direction. But one of these rebelled and formed a government in the wilderness. Some Aymara forces became his allies. Others attempted to become independent—as they had been before conquest by the Incas. However, the Aymara, who often fought among themselves, never challenged the Spanish as a single group. By 1538 Pizarro's brothers Gonzalo and Hernando conquered the altiplano and montaña. There the Spaniards founded towns, including La Paz, Cochabamba, Oruro, and Chuquisaca (the early name for Sucre). The territory officially became the Audiencia of Charcas (after one of the Aymara kingdoms), but it was commonly known as Upper Peru. Inca resistance never took the land back, and the last rebel Inca was captured and executed in 1572.

The Spaniards brought new technology and animals to Upper Peru. Iron tools, looms, and Spanish-type plows arrived. Sheep, chickens, pigs, and cattle followed the horses brought by Pizarro. Meat, along with new crops like alfalfa, improved the diet in the territory. The improvements, however, did not change the fact that the Aymara- and Quechua-speaking people of Upper Peru had become subjects of Spanish rulers.

To the Spanish they were "Indians." The new masters in Upper Peru did not want to exterminate or expel the native people, the plan followed by later settlers in some other parts of North and South America.

The Spanish introduced a new wool-bearing animal to the altiplano—the sheep.   Doranne
Jacobson

Instead, they forced the Indians to perform the menial or hard labor that kept any sixteenth-century society running. Someone, for example, had to carry water and harvest crops. The Spanish considered such work demeaning and avoided it whenever possible. The Aymara and Quechua Indians were used as farm laborers, household servants and miners— especially miners.

The Silver Mountain

The reason for forming Spanish colonies in the Americas, after all, was to enrich Spain with the wealth of the new lands. Inca artworks proved there were precious metals in the Andes, and—after pillaging the Inca art treasures—the Spanish began to explore the land.

In April 1545 explorers entered the eastern range of the Andes at a point southeast of Lake Poopó. They discovered a picturesque mountain standing above the rest of the country. It was so symmetrical that later religious paintings portrayed it as the gown of the Virgin. Stretching for a hundred yards along the face of the mountain was an outcropping of rock. The Spaniards discovered that this was a vein of silver ore of incredible purity. In the Western Hemisphere there had never had there been such a rich silver discovery, and there has never been another since.

They called it Potosí. Within weeks, 175 Spaniards with 3,000 Indian laborers reached the area to stake claims. They faced windstorms, freezing temperatures, and a shortage of oxygen on the 16,000-foot (5,000-meter) mountain. It didn't matter. A new town, also called

Inca silver artworks like this alpaca excited Spaniards in search of riches. Neg. no. 337198, Department of Library Services, American Museum of Natural History

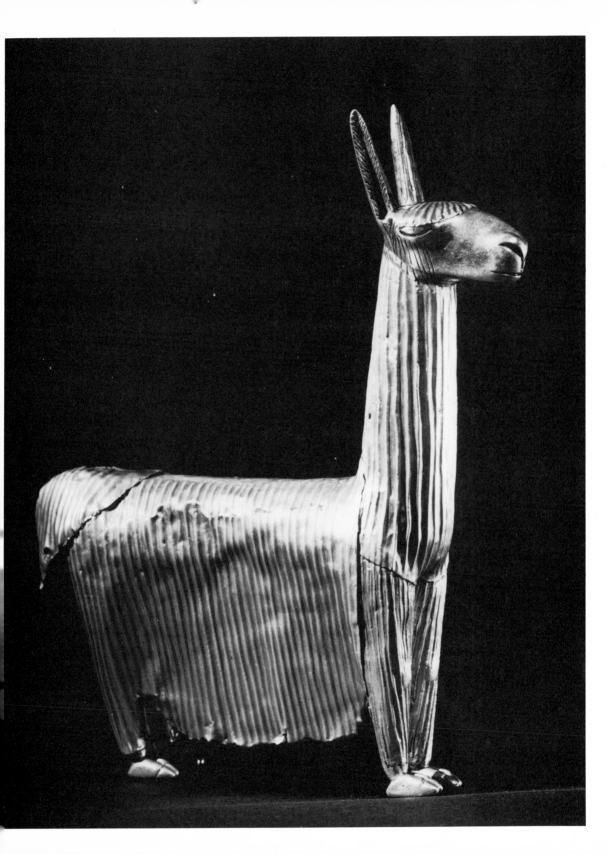

Potosí, sprang up nearby on the altiplano. Within eighteen months it held 2,500 houses and 14,000 people.

Many expected the silver to run out quickly. Exactly that happened with the rich ore near the surface. Veins deeper in the mountain proved difficult to refine, and the growth of Potosí slowed for a time. But there was too much silver to ignore. Spanish authorities learned of a new way to refine the ore using mercury. They saw to it that mercury was mined in Peru and transported to Potosí's refineries. The incredible mines began to prosper again.

By 1600 Potosí was one of the richest cities in the world. In 1597 a bride from a particularly wealthy Potosí family brought her husband a dowry of 2.3 million pesos, an enormous fortune. City residents decorated their homes with German ironware, Dutch linens, Egyptian rugs, and Chinese ivory. They imported French beaver hats to protect themselves from the cold. It seems incredible that such luxuries were transported from all over the world to the inaccessible highlands of Upper Peru. But it was possible because merchants could sell goods in the city for ten times what they had cost to buy. Potosí also became one of the largest cities in the world, with a population of 160,000 in the early seventeenth century. Its coat of arms carried this motto:

I am rich Potosí,
Treasure of the world,
The king of all mountains,
And the envy of all kings.

The silver mountain fulfilled the dreams of the Spanish monarchs. In those days, a nation's wealth was measured by the volume of precious metals in its royal treasury. So each year, a huge caravan of ships assembled in the Caribbean to carry the king's share of the American riches back to Spain. Until about 1750, more than half the silver from the South American colonies came from Potosí.

The mountain and the city helped establish mining as the principal industry of Upper Peru. During Spanish rule the colony's mines produced about 25,000 tons (23,000 metric tons) of silver—enough to make half a dozen sterling silver teapots for every Bolivian alive today.

Spaniard and Indian

Working mines before the invention of power tools was extremely strenuous labor, requiring the services of up to 13,500 Indians at a time. The high altitude and cold made the work all the more difficult. Candles provided the only light deep in the mines. They also filled the air with smoke, and the thin air was already clogged with dust and the smell of human waste. An Indian might be forced to carry a heavy bucket of ore hundreds of feet up a mine shaft. In semidarkness, he would climb ropes and feel out toeholds notched in logs. Drenched with sweat, he would then emerge into freezing wind at the mouth of the mine. Accidents, deadly gas, and the combination of hard labor, malnutrition, and disease killed thousands of laborers. Some Indian mothers deliberately crippled their sons to save them from the Spanish mines.To guarantee a large enough work force, Spanish authorities imposed the *mita* system in mining areas. This required one seventh of the men from each Indian town to work in the mines.

Indians labored for Spanish lords in many other ways. The people of cities like Potosí needed to be fed, so agriculture and trade expanded in Upper Peru. In turn, the ancient trade between the altiplano and the montaña increased. Indians were needed to lead and care for pack animals on the trade roads. They worked on plantations near Co-

This drawing of Indian miners at Potosí appeared in an illustrated atlas of the world around 1730.   National Anthropological Archives/Smithsonian Institution

chabamba and ranches on the altiplano. Women served as cooks, maids, and personal servants throughout Upper Peru.

Like Indian miners, these laborers were not technically slaves, but the Spanish found ways to force them into service. Indian labor was one of the few things in Upper Peru that the early conquistadores valued. Like silver, it meant wealth—and personal wealth was very much on their minds. The conquistadores had not been wealthy men in the Old World, and they demanded a reward for bringing new lands into the Spanish empire. Some of them were granted rights called *encomiendas* by the Spanish monarchy. An *encomienda* gave the holder the right to demand labor tribute from Indians in a given area.

Encomiendas lasted only for a specified length of time; the system disappeared before long. Later Spaniards became the owners of *haciendas*. On these large estates, Indians were allowed to have small plots for their own purposes. In turn, though, they owed a labor tribute to the *hacienda* owner. Indians were also subject to taxation. They had to pay either in goods they made themselves or in silver earned working for the Spanish. All these systems were designed to turn Indian labor into Spanish wealth.

Supposedly, the Indians got something in return. Spaniards receiving *encomiendas* and owning *haciendas* were responsible for the protection and Christianization of Indians. In practice, though, the welfare of Indians was largely ignored.

Finally, the Spaniards encouraged coca chewing among all Indians. Earlier coca had only been used by the well-to-do, such as the Inca royal family. As trade with the montaña expanded, coca became plentiful enough for all Indians on the altiplano. The mild narcotic in the coca leaves lessened the discomfort of a hard life, perhaps making the Indians a little more willing to accept it. That was just what the Spanish wanted.

There were frequent Indian revolts, even after the death of the last rebel Inca in 1572. But for more than two centuries these were all local

Beyond the Spanish Islands

The Spanish and creoles of Upper Peru mostly stayed in the cities, which historians later called Spanish islands. The newcomers did not stamp out Indian culture.

The traditional lives of Aymara and Quechua Indians *were* changed by the Spaniard. They had had to labor in the Inca's fields, but their rulers had been careful to compensate work and to see to it that families were provided for when members were absent. The Spanish cared less about such things. And they were much more interested in the crippling and killing mine labor that wasted so many men.

In rural areas, though, native tradition lived on. Indians, usually women, spun thread from raw wool and made cloth, all by hand. A woman might take a full year to make one set of clothes for her entire family. Both men and women spent long hours planting,

uprisings, none involving very many Indians. Colonial authorities easily defeated them all.

The Spanish successfully governed Aymara and Quechua Indians in Upper Peru, but they were less successful in spreading their religion to these new subjects. The Indians seemed willing to become Christians, allowing priests to baptize them, for example. But they steadfastly refused to drop their own religious practices. A few Dominicans and later the Jesuits tried to stamp these out, but they never succeeded. The main problem was that there were few priests in Upper Peru, and most of those were notoriously unassertive.

growing, and harvesting crops. Adobe walls had to be constructed for huts, then roofs thatched and mud packed for floors. There also remained the endless task of watching flocks. The number of alpacas, llamas, or sheep a family owned determined its wealth. Long after the Incas, Indians continued to tie knots into *quipus* to keep count of their animals.

Life was not all toil. Men beat drums and played flutes at ancient annual festivals. Herbal cures passed from generation to generation. Spaniards had imposed Christianity, but Indians had hardly become orthodox believers. The Aymara, for example, continued to tow girls across fields before planting, a fertility ritual that had nothing do with Christianity. The personal contact that a priest normally has with a congregation did not exist in Upper Peru. A priest only rarely visited any particular *hacienda* or Indian town.

Those few Spaniards who did live in or visit the country ruled through local Indian leaders or overseers. The only descendants of Spain that most Indians encountered were sheep.

A few active priests made significant contributions. Some defended Indian welfare. The Jesuits studied the Aymara language and became the first to write it down. But most priests exploited the Indians in the same way other Spaniards did. On infrequent visits to rural estates or Aymara and Quechua communities, they performed marriages and baptisms, collected stiff fees, and departed quickly.

The Indian population of Upper Peru declined severely under Spanish rule. At the time of the conquest, many Aymara and Quechua Indians died in battle. Far more died in the mines or from epidemics, brought from Europe, of diseases against which they had no immunity.

Some may have simply fled the region, migrating to areas still outside Spanish control. After this sharp drop, the population continued to decline gradually for nearly two centuries. The fact that the Indian population did not recover in these years shows what hard lives the people lived. A new epidemic around 1720 caused another rapid drop. After that the population held steady for the remaining century of Spanish rule. The virtual disappearance of native people that occurred in some parts of the Americas did not take place in Upper Peru.

Meanwhile the Spanish population climbed. About 70,000 Spaniards immigrated to the former Inca empire. Artisans and merchants followed the adventurers. Early on, the great majority of the newcomers to Upper Peru were men. Because most could not find Spanish wives, they took Indian wives. This practice was common and perfectly proper in the eyes of the Spanish. (In later English colonies in North America, the marriage of a European to an Indian was considered highly unusual, even sinful.)

Even though Spaniards mixed freely with native people throughout their empire, they remained very conscious of race. Race had a more complex meaning in Spanish America than it does today. Place of birth affected the way a person was viewed. For example, when a man and a woman born in Spain had a child born in Upper Peru, the child would be called a *creole.* A Spaniard would consider such a person to be of an inferior race because he or she had been born in an inferior country.

A man with both Indian and Spanish blood was called a *mestizo* or a *cholo.* A woman was a *mestiza* or *chola.* But again, people were classified by more than just bloodlines. The Spanish idea of race had as much to do with people's language, dress, and manners as it did with their parents. Because these things can change, a person could sometimes change his or her race. One traveler around 1770 explained how this might work for an Indian man: If he washes his face, cuts his hair and nails, and puts on a clean shirt, he can become a cholo. Then if he gets Spanish clothes and shoes, he can begin passing as a mestizo within a few months.

The Spanish had dozens of racial classifications. African slaves brought to the Americas made things even more complicated. The English and Portugese also brought Africans to their American colonies, and a large population of blacks grew in North America, the Caribbean, and Brazil.

Few came to Upper Peru, partly because of the expense of transporting them so far. A tiny number arrived as household slaves. The Spanish also tried using black slaves in the Potosí mines. But the Africans had never lived at extreme altitude, and they died even faster than the highland Indians when forced into severe labor. As a result, nearly everyone in Upper Peru had a bloodline that flowed from Spain, the Inca empire, or both. And even though the Indian population eventually dropped to one fifth what it had once been, Indians remained a large majority in the colony.

A Changing World

From the conquest until about 1750, Spain ruled Upper Peru without major conflict. From the Spanish point of view, the colony had worked well for more than two centuries. Most important, it had poured a fortune in silver into the Spanish treasury. Spain had maintained an eastern town, Santa Cruz, since 1561, though it had never extended Spanish rule to the eastern Indians. However, even here it seemed they might succeed. By 1750 Jesuit missionaries were making regular contact with lowland peoples.

But gradual changes in both the colony and the rest of the world were bringing the colonial era to an end. In the colony silver production had been falling since 1650. The remaining treasure in the silver mountain was much harder to mine than the exhausted surface veins. The population of Potosí had fallen to one fifth what it once had been. Explorers never succeeded in finding the new wealth supposedly hidden in fabulous jungle cities; these were just myths. Then, in 1767, Jesuits were expelled from the entire Spanish empire, and the contacts with eastern Indians were lost. In the 1780's, a Quechua Indian named Tupac Amaru claimed to be a new Inca ruler. He began an Indian uprising that disrupted Upper Peru and other Spanish colonies. Before he was defeated, *haciendas* were sacked, isolated towns were attacked, and La Paz itself was twice besieged by Indian armies.

Outside, Spain was not the world power it once had been. The Portugese colony of Brazil seemed to threaten Spanish lands south of Upper Peru. Britain's navy had become so powerful that it threatened Spain's contact with its colonies. And France was building a powerful army on the European mainland. At this critical time, a weak king inherited the Spanish throne.

The late eighteenth century was a complex time rich with new ideas. It would be called the Enlightenment, and many of its leaders questioned the authority of popes and monarchs. Thought turned to action. In North America thirteen colonies violently rebelled against British rule and became the United States. In France a bloody revolution overthrew the monarchy and killed the royal family.

Early in the nineteenth century France's new ruler, Napoleon Bonaparte, attempted to conquer Europe. The Frenchman's army intimidated the Spanish royal family and forced its abdication. In 1808 Napoleon crowned his brother Joseph as king of Spain. Joseph Bonaparte naturally assumed that he also ruled the Spanish empire in America. He sent his own officials to take over in the colonies. But with Napoleon's army spread across Europe, he could never have supplied the men to enforce his brother's rule over the Caribbean, Mexico, Central America, and South America. When Joseph's officials arrived, the Spanish Americans refused to recognize their authority and sent them back home.

For a while Spanish America remained loyal to the deposed Spanish royal family, but it was no longer under stable European rule.

A Republic
from Colonial Ruins

Nine years before Napoleon overthrew the Spanish monarchy, a sixteen-year-old creole arrived in Madrid to complete his education. He was an intelligent boy from Caracas, a member of one of the wealthiest families in South America. He was used to being treated with respect. But his hosts never let him forget that they considered creoles to be inferior.

The Spanish snubbed even wealthy creoles, sarcastically calling them "cocoa grandees" (because some creoles in the Caribbean had made fortunes selling cocoa). The teenager got into trouble when he drew his sword after hearing a Spanish officer ridicule Americans. A popular joke in Madrid added to his discomfort: If a donkey driver was the last person alive in Spain, he would be the only one fit to rule America—except perhaps for the donkey.

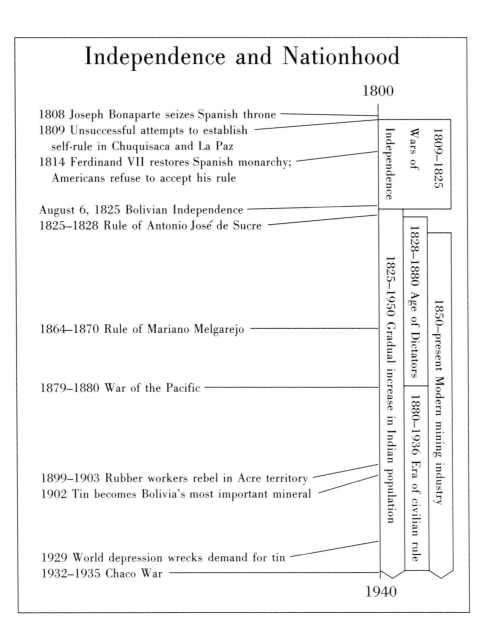

Independence and Nationhood

1800

1808 Joseph Bonaparte seizes Spanish throne

1809 Unsuccessful attempts to establish
self-rule in Chuquisaca and La Paz

1814 Ferdinand VII restores Spanish monarchy;
Americans refuse to accept his rule

August 6, 1825 Bolivian Independence

1825–1828 Rule of Antonio José de Sucre

1864–1870 Rule of Mariano Melgarejo

1879–1880 War of the Pacific

1899–1903 Rubber workers rebel in Acre territory

1902 Tin becomes Bolivia's most important mineral

1929 World depression wrecks demand for tin

1932–1935 Chaco War

1809–1825 Wars of Independence

1828–1880 Age of Dictators

1880–1936 Era of civilian rule

1825–1950 Gradual increase in Indian population

1850–present Modern mining industry

1940

What the creole student learned in the capital of the Spanish empire was no joke. King Carlos IV seemed more interested in outdoor leisure than in government. Queen María Luisa used her vicious temper to dominate him. And everyone repeated a rumor—almost certainly true—that the timid king's unpopular first minister was the queen's lover.

The youth, Simón Bolívar, went home convinced that South Americans would be better off ruling themselves.

Independence

After Carlos was deposed by Napoleon in 1808, the king's officials still ran Spanish America and controlled a royal army already there. These were the forces creole leaders like Bolívar would have to defeat to win independence.

Upper Peru was the first colony to declare independence, but it would be the last to win it. In 1809 creoles in Chuquisaca and La Paz claimed the right to rule themselves since there was no legitimate king in Spain. They said they were still loyal to the deposed royal family, but not to Spanish officials in America. Their actions signaled the beginning of South America's Wars of Independence. Royal troops (those loyal to Spain) from Buenos Aires quickly crushed the revolt in Chuquisaca, and troops from Lima defeated the dissidents in La Paz. Upper Peru's creoles continued to spread ideas about nationhood, but they were no longer the leaders in the fight.

In 1810 creole leaders in Caracas, Bogotá, Buenos Aires, Santiago, and western Mexico all rebelled. They also claimed loyalty to the deposed royal family, but many really wanted independence. All these movements were put down by royal forces except the one in Buenos Aires. There creoles established Argentina as an independent nation.

For the next fifteen years, royal forces and independence forces struggled for control of Spanish areas of South America. In 1814 Napoleon was defeated and Ferdinand VII (the son of Carlos) recovered his family's throne in Spain. South Americans now had to decide whether they really were loyal subjects as most had been saying all along.

Many decided they were not, and the Wars of Independence continued. Peru was especially loyal to Spain, but Argentina remained independent. Upper Peru was caught between these two stronger regions, and both fought to control it. For six years its cities were sacked repeatedly, and its mines were wrecked. An Argentine army even looted the royal mint at Potosí. Peru finally took control—but not for long.

Peru received little support from Spain, and it became increasingly alone as independence forces grew stronger both to the north and to the south. In 1817 José de San Martín marched 5,600 men westward from Argentina to oppose Spanish rule. Following a difficult strategy, he passed south of Upper Peru and marched his army through 12,000-foot (3,600-meter) passes in the Andes. Royal forces on the other side were taken by surprise, and within a year Chile became another independent nation.

From the north came Simón Bolívar, by then a highly respected leader of the independence movement. He assembled an army near the Caribbean coast and brought it south along the Andes. In 1819, Gran Colombia was independent. (This large nation later split into modern-day Colombia, Ecuador, and Venezuela.) For the next five years Peru and Upper Peru were the only Spanish areas in South America. Finally, in December 1824, a general in Bolívar's army launched a final drive through the highlands. Antonio José de Sucre led independence forces against royal forces camped at Ayacucho, a Peruvian town between Lima and Cuzco. In a short, violent battle in the high Andes, Sucre's

Simón Bolívar (on white horse) directs the 1819 Battle of Boyacá in Gran Colombia. His victory isolated royal forces in Peru and Upper Peru. Organization of American States

force defeated the much larger royal force. The Battle of Ayacucho was the last major action of the Wars of Independence. Sucre then took his army into Upper Peru and ended Spanish rule on the continent without major resistance.

Bolívar, revered as the Liberator, believed Upper Peru should become part of Argentina. But the creoles there wanted nationhood, and Sucre supported them. To win over Bolívar, they invited him to write the constitution and they named the country in his honor. Bolívar gave in, and the Republic of Bolivia was born on August 6, 1825.

The Fabric of Dictatorship

"Whom do you trust?" a visitor is said to have asked a nineteenth-century Bolivian dictator.

Mariano Melgarejo did not answer right away. Instead, he took off his shirt and threw it onto the floor. Then he drew his pistol and fired a bullet through the crumpled garment. Finally he spoke:

"I trust not even my shirt."

Probably this is only a tall tale. But it reveals something about how Melgarejo and other South American *caudillos* held power.

These men might be violent and ignorant, but they had mesmerizing personalities. They could inspire—or terrify—to the point that people would accept them as leaders. Stories like the one above added to their power. Personalities replaced constitutions. *Caudillos* did not just lead governments; they *became* governments, insisting on unquestioned authority for themselves.

Personality did not make them invulnerable, however. Melgarejo was overthrown after six years.

Difficulties and Division

As Bolivia's first constitutional president, Sucre tried to establish a democratic government that included a congress and courts. But Bolivians weren't used to a system that shared a ruler's power. When they thought of government, they pictured kings, popes—even Incas. All were men who had ruled with total authority. On paper, Bolivia was a modern democracy. But after Sucre, it was to be ruled by a series of dictators until 1880.

These dictators or *caudillos* often seized power by force after gaining a following in the military. One early *caudillo* threw out Bolívar's constitution and enacted his own. Later he invaded Peru to try to extend his rule. Another took power by personally killing his predecessor. The *caudillos* had little understanding of government or economics. They could be cruel, and none treated Indians as full citizens. Sucre had abolished the colonial head tax on Indians, but it was reimposed. One *caudillo* even tried to seize the land of free Indian communities so he could sell it back to them.

The chaos of Bolivia's early governments left the nation unable to solve a serious problem it had faced from the start. Three centuries of colonial digging had stripped its mountains of the ore that was easiest to reach. Mining what remained was difficult and required the latest equipment. For example, thousands of Bolivia's mines were flooded, a common problem in deep shafts. By this time, steam pumps could drain water from mines, but Bolivia didn't have the money to buy them.

Miners dug out what little ore they could reach with old methods. They even looked for the last traces of silver in old slag piles (the dirt and rock separated from the silver when ore is processed). But for

Antonio José de Sucre.   Organization of American States

Chuquisaca, renamed Sucre in 1840, as it appeared shortly after independence. Neg. no. 320337, Department of Library Services, American Museum of Natural History

decades, silver failed to bring in enough money to modernize the mines. Bolivia faced a frustrating situation. The soil held a fortune in mineral wealth, but the country was too poor to reach it. The decline of Potosí was the clearest sign of trouble. In 1825 it remained the country's largest mining center. Yet its population was only 9,000—down from 160,000 two centuries earlier.

Mining, Bolivia's only major industry, clearly could not support the majority of the people. Throughout the nineteenth century, nine out of ten Bolivians lived off the land outside the cities. Some whites (creoles and former Spaniards) owned country estates, but they were a tiny minority in the countryside. Most rural people were Aymara and Quechua Indians, who supported themselves by raising crops and animals and by trading between the altiplano and the montaña. They survived the way their ancestors had during colonial times and before.

Most Indians had no feeling that they were part of a new nation called Bolivia. They had to pay the Indian head tax and provide labor as they had before. But whites still controlled them through Indian overseers on *haciendas* or through chiefs in Indian communities. Most Indians had little personal contact with whites. Their own languages, music, dance, dress, and customs endured. Visits by priests continued to be rare, and Indian festivals and religious practices lived on.

One thing did change, perhaps because of the reduced demand for severe labor in the mines. For whatever reason, more Indians were surviving and reproducing. The decline of the colonial period was reversed, and the Indian population began to grow gradually. Bolivia, unlike most American nations, continued to have a huge Indian majority.

Most whites, in turn, remained isolated in the cities. A lot of trading took place with the country (the urban people, after all, had to be fed). La Paz and Cochabamba remained the country's largest cities because they were centers for this trade. But *cholos* conducted most of this commerce, and the separation between whites and Indians continued.

Silver and Tin

During the 1850's and 1860's Bolivia finally managed to get modern equipment into its silver mines. Steam pumps drained shafts, and silver revenue increased. By the end of the century, Bolivian mines were as well equipped as any in the world. Silver production climbed higher than ever, even beating the colonial glory days of Potosí.

More important in the long run, Bolivia began selling a new product from its mines—tin. The earliest colonial miners had known the Andes held rich veins of tin. But "rich" was not a word the Spanish would have used. Tin had little value in those days. There was certainly no profit in shipping it abroad. That changed in the last years of the nineteenth

This 1872 silver boliviano is about the size of an old-style U.S. silver dollar. Bolivia's seal (detail) incorporates the sun, the mountain at Potosí, a llama, and a bundle of grain. Both photos David Nelson Blair

century. Growing industries in large nations needed Bolivia's tin. For example, the booming food-packaging industry in Great Britain required raw material for millions of tin cans. Early in the twentieth century tin surpassed silver as Bolivia's most important mineral.

Government after 1880 also improved. Incompetent *caudillos* had disgraced themselves in a costly war with Chile. A new constitution passed. Soon elected civilian presidents were encouraging the construction of railroads and telegraph lines. Political parties competed for power, and presidents were overthrown when public and government opponents believed election fraud had taken place. Even these upheavals involved little bloodshed, and Bolivia enjoyed a long era of peace and stability.

Prosperity and democracy, however, did not come to most Bolivians. The nation's population reached 1.6 million in 1900, but laws prevented all but about 30,000 to 40,000 from voting. The country's wealthiest families, who owned the *haciendas* and controlled the mining industry, were able to control political leaders. This ruling class became known as the *rosca*. It used the government to enrich its own members. For example, the new rail and telegraph lines served the mine owners, not ordinary people. The government was not concerned with new roads or schools that could have raised living standards for the majority of Bolivians.

The growth of the Indian population may have been a sign of slightly better conditions, but it also created problems. Free Indian towns owned community lands, but with the population on the rise, many more Indians were forced to move onto *haciendas.* New laws also let *hacienda* owners buy up community lands. Thus the power of the *haciendas* grew while the amount of Indian land fell.

Prosperity for some turned into prosperity for almost none by 1930.

The Great Depression drastically reduced industry in the United States, Britain, Germany, and other industrial countries. These nations had been Bolivia's biggest customers for tin—but no more. Since it had no other major industry, Bolivia faced a severe financial crisis.

Lost Lands

The price of tin was only one of the problems Bolivia faced in dealing with other nations. Since independence, powerful South American nations hoped to extend their rule into undeveloped territories—just as the United States did in the nineteenth century when it annexed much of Mexico. Bolivia claimed vast undeveloped territories, especially in the east. But borders had never been formally set, and other countries claimed some of the same lands.

Portugal's former empire in South America had remained a single country—Brazil. It became Bolivia's largest and most powerful neighbor. The border with Brazil ran for hundreds of miles, but exactly where was it? It passed through tropical plains and jungles, and no one had ever marked it off. In 1868, Bolivia asked Brazil for a treaty allowing it to use Brazil's rivers to ship goods to the Atlantic Ocean. Brazil appeared happy to help, but it insisted on settling border questions in the same treaty. Bolivia had to agree to an "adjustment" of its territory. Brazil got 40,000 square miles (104,000 square kilometers) that Bolivia had previously claimed.

Thirty years later a rubber boom brought many Brazilians into a northern jungle region of Bolivia. Since virtually no Bolivians had settled the territory, Brazilians quickly became a majority. Bolivia hoped to profit by taxing rubber shipped to Brazil, but Brazilians in the territory rebelled. Bolivia could not regain control, and in 1903 it

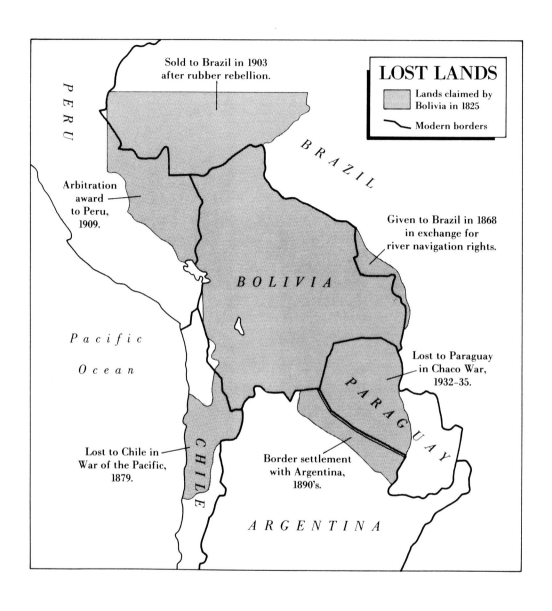

LOST LANDS

Sold to Brazil in 1903 after rubber rebellion.

Lands claimed by Bolivia in 1825

Modern borders

PERU

BRAZIL

Arbitration award to Peru, 1909.

Given to Brazil in 1868 in exchange for river navigation rights.

BOLIVIA

Pacific

Ocean

Lost to Paraguay in Chaco War, 1932–35.

PARAGUAY

Lost to Chile in War of the Pacific, 1879.

CHILE

Border settlement with Argentina, 1890's.

ARGENTINA

agreed to sell the land to Brazil for a token price.

Bolivia's most humiliating losses, though, came at the hands of its Spanish-speaking neighbors. In colonial times, borders between the colonies didn't matter much since all the territories belonged to Spain anyway. That changed after independence. Bolivia's experience with Brazil had been preceded by a similar dispute with Chile.

Bolivia owned a strip of desert along the Pacific coast that gave the country its only direct access to the sea. Without a port, Bolivia would have to export raw materials and import foreign goods through other countries. That usually meant paying duties. In the 1870's, silver and nitrite deposits were discovered along Bolivia's coast. Chilean workers rushed to work the mines and, like the Brazilians in the jungle, soon became a majority in Bolivian territory. In 1879 they rebelled when Bolivia tried to tax them. This gave Chile an excuse to expand northward. Ready with its army and navy, it quickly defeated Bolivia in the War of the Pacific. Bolivia never regained a direct outlet to the sea.

Not only did the nation lose land to powerful neighbors, it lost land to a weak neighbor. Bolivia and Paraguay both claimed the Chaco region southeast of Santa Cruz. Until the twentieth century, however, war over the barren region didn't seem worthwhile. Discovery of oil changed the situation. In 1932 Bolivian President Daniel Salamanca provoked a border skirmish in hopes of quickly taking the entire territory. Instead he brought his nation disaster. Three years later, Paraguay had most of the Chaco, and a humiliated Bolivia was beginning to understand what it had cost:

—52,000 Bolivians were dead.
—The country owed $230 million in war debts.
—A military government had arrested Salamanca, and more than fifty years of civilian rule were ending.

In 1932, the nation had faced economic difficulties because the world demand for tin had collapsed. In 1935, it was no better off. But the Chaco War had added death, debt, and dictatorship to the country's trauma. No nation could endure such deeply felt shocks without change, and Bolivia was ready for a new beginning.

Toward
a Modern Nation

Bolivian Indians drafted into the Chaco War wore pouches on their belts. On one side they held stewed corn called *mote*, and on the other side they carried coca leaves. Most of these soldiers spoke only Aymara or Quechua, and to make commands understandable, officers called out "mote" and "coca" because the men did not know the Spanish words for "left" and "right."

Indians accounted for most of Bolivia's war dead, but their sacrifice did not immediately change the status of their people. Through the 1940's, they were denied participation in national affairs. Most could not even cast ballots because voting required literacy in Spanish. Yet the Chaco War opened a period of discontent for both Indian and white

Bolivians. Ultimately it led to one of the most important revolutions in Latin American history.

Conditions before 1952

Landless laborers in rural Bolivia lived hard lives with no luxuries. These Quechua and Aymara Indians who worked for wealthy landowners under the *hacienda* system introduced centuries earlier by the Spanish were called *colonos*. Their identification as *indios* was in itself a barrier to improvement in their lives. *Indio*, the Spanish word for "Indian," carried extremely vulgar connotations not present in the English form. Indians were stereotyped as gloomy, hostile, suspicious, treacherous, and vindictive. Worse yet, whites sometimes called them *"indiobrutos."* This implied what some Europeans had argued four hundred years earlier: Indians were just brutish work animals that could be treated like oxen or donkeys. One of Bolivia's ministers of education commented on the people who made up most of his country's population: "We don't understand his forms of life nor his mental mechanism. . . . The Indian does not allow himself to be understood, he doesn't desire communication."

The homes of *colonos* resembled those of colonial times. Families had no sanitary facilities, and no doctors practiced in many rural areas. Instead, they used Indian curers, and on some *haciendas* six babies in ten died in their first year. Formal education did not exist. A 1929 law required large *haciendas* to set up schools, but it was ignored. Landowners, called *patróns*, believed that education would give their *colonos* skills they might take elsewhere, thus threatening the *hacienda* system.

On the altiplano, a man might be allowed a small plot of land for his own use, often the land his father had worked. He used the same simple

Bolivian Governments Since 1931

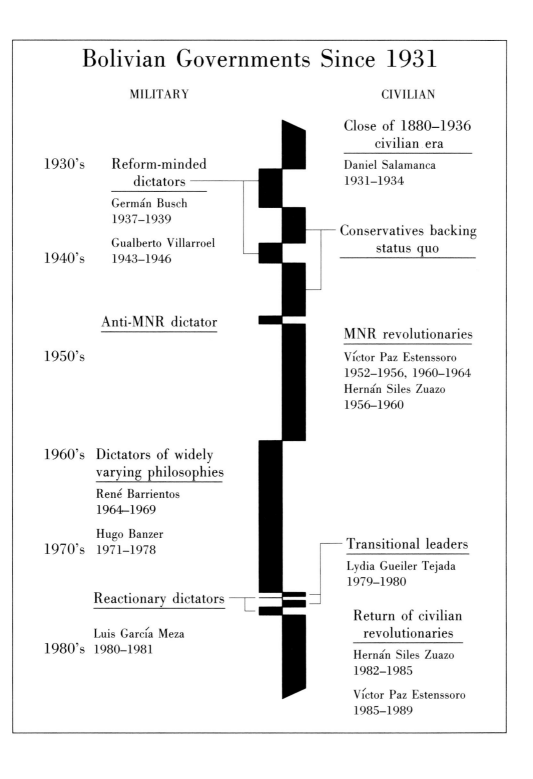

MILITARY   CIVILIAN

Close of 1880–1936
civilian era

1930's   Reform-minded   Daniel Salamanca
          dictators   1931–1934

          Germán Busch
          1937–1939

          Gualberto Villarroel   Conservatives backing
1940's   1943–1946   status quo

          Anti-MNR dictator
                                 MNR revolutionaries

1950's   Víctor Paz Estenssoro
                                 1952–1956, 1960–1964
                                 Hernán Siles Zuazo
                                 1956–1960

1960's   Dictators of widely
          varying philosophies
          René Barrientos
          1964–1969

          Hugo Banzer   Transitional leaders
1970's   1971–1978
                                 Lydia Gueiler Tejada
                                 1979–1980

          Reactionary dictators
                                 Return of civilian
                                 revolutionaries
          Luis García Meza
1980's   1980–1981   Hernán Siles Zuazo
                                 1982–1985

                                 Víctor Paz Estenssoro
                                 1985–1989

tools his ancestors had. A *colono* family might also have seven or eight sheep, a cow, a pig, and a couple of burros, and would raise them on its own plot or on a common field, whichever was the custom on the particular *hacienda*. Often families did not have enough to feed themselves properly.

In exchange for the use of plots, a *colono* owed labor to the landowners. Able-bodied Indians, both men and women, might spend three or four days a week working in a *patrón*'s fields or tending his large herds. Obligations did not end there. *Colonos* were also required to perform a number of services. For example, a man might work for a week tending the mules of the landowner. A woman might have to cook for the *patrón*'s administrator. If the *patrón* had another hacienda in the *yungas* or a house in the city, men and women might have to work there, spending up to a year away from their families.

The altiplano landowners were supposedly responsible for the welfare of the families on their *haciendas*, but usually they only provided liquor for feast days and passed out rations of coca. Many of them did not even live on the *haciendas*, leaving administrators in charge and giving virtually nothing in exchange for the incomes they collected.

Laborers in the *yungas* were slightly better off because there was a greater demand for their services. Thus, *patróns* were willing to provide more to attract them. A new *colono* family might not have to perform services until it was established, for example. In addition, landowners generally had fewer grazing animals that their workers had to tend, and in some instances, they paid the workers a little for their work. Nonetheless, essentially the same relationship existed between the *yungas colono* and *patrón*. A man might be required to receive and dry the coca brought from the fields. A woman might have to spin thread from lamb's wool and make bags and blankets for the *patrón*.

Indians had no recourse if they were mistreated. Bolivia's legal system normally stayed out of *hacienda* affairs. *Patróns* dictated the law on their lands. They controlled the people there through their administrators and Indian overseers, and cruelty and intimidation were a part of life. In one case, a Quechua overseer beat his own father when the older man got tired during a harvest. In another, an Aymara man was evicted because he was suspected of losing a mule.

Exploitation of Indians took place beyond the *hacienda* as well. In the mining industry, for example, conditions for the workers were at least as bad. Most miners of the era worked for one of three huge private tin companies, the largest owned by Simón Patiño. This native of the Cochabamba Valley made a vast fortune, but never used the wealth to modernize mines, build roads, or otherwise improve conditions in his own country. Instead, he invested his money in Europe, where he lived the last twenty years of his life, becoming one of the richest men in the world. Bolivians, sensitive to the fact that their silver had been shipped abroad in colonial years, felt betrayed that Patiño was doing the same with their tin wealth.

The comparison caused particular bitterness because the workers in the Bolivian mines occupied cramped company lodgings that were packed together in long rows. Often two families lived in one room. The mines took a great toll. Miners risked being maimed or killed by gas, explosions, or cave-ins. Worst of all, they suffered from a lung disease called silicosis. Thus, the youngest miners usually performed the most strenuous tasks, such as running hand-held drills. It was expected that they would sicken as they got older, and when they did, they moved to other jobs, such as loading and pushing the carts that moved the ore up the shafts. The extreme altitude of most mines aggravated the lung condition, and frequently miners died before the age of thirty-five.

Justice

Even before the Chaco War, a few white Bolivians had become concerned about Indians. One of them was Ricardo Jaimes Freyre (1872–1933), a diplomat and one of Bolivia's most important writers. White treatment of Indians is bluntly portrayed in this dialogue from one of his short stories. An Indian is confronting a white traveler:

"Señor . . . let me have my horse."

"Again, you imbecile! Do you want me to travel on foot? I gave you mine in exchange, and that's enough."

"But your horse is dead."

"Of course he's dead, but that's because I made him run fifteen hours at a stretch. He was a great horse! Yours is worthless. Do you think he'll last many hours?"

From Ricardo Jaimes Freyre, "Indian Justice," in *Classic Tales from Spanish America*, edited and translated by William E. Colford (Great Neck, NY: Barron's, 1962), p. 46.

A Popular Revolt

Fighting the Chaco War had temporarily placed exploited and ignored Indians into the service of the nation. Many felt that they had been used, often by cowardly and incompetent commanders, just as they had been used by wealthy *patróns* or mine owners. It was not only Indians who believed this; *cholo* and white merchants, professionals, office workers, and university students gradually began to question the inferior status of Indians. A few had seen this abuse firsthand during the war. More read new novels that emphasized the wartime injustices.

Indians were not the only beneficiaries of these new sympathies. Another group of Bolivians had long been treated as less than full citizens. Women could own land and property; some wealthy white women even inherited *haciendas.* But they could not vote. After the Chaco War, urban organizations formed to give all Bolivian women that right.

The years 1935 to 1952 saw a struggle for change. The war had given Indians a much better understanding of politics, and they began to join agricultural and mine unions. New political parties denounced injustice. Meanwhile, military dictators became leaders in the struggle for reform. One of them, Gualberto Villarroel, called a national Indian congress in 1945. He tried unsuccessfully to abolish the system of compulsory labor that exploited Indians.

But these were also times of economic and political chaos. The nation's financial health still depended on the tin industry, and it shifted between depression and relative prosperity as world demand for tin fluctuated. Rule passed between the military reformists and conservative civilians. A new constitution was enacted and then suspended within a year. Villarroel was killed by a mob, and an earlier reformist dictator committed suicide.

In 1951 the country elected as president Víctor Paz Estenssoro, the exiled leader of one of the new parties, the Nationalist Revolutionary Movement. (The Spanish name is Movimiento Nacionalista Revolucionario, and in both English and Spanish it is abbreviated as the MNR.) The president-elect prepared to return to Bolivia, but the outgoing president was determined to stop the MNR from taking power. Though he was a civilian, he turned the government over to a military dictator so that Paz Estenssoro could not take office. By this time, however, the

MNR had extensive popular support. When night fell over La Paz in the hours after the military takeover, carefully built fires appeared on the hillsides overlooking the city. The flames spelled out M-N-R.

A few months later, just before dawn on April 9, 1952, machine-gun fire erupted in La Paz, and a civil war began across the country. In three days of fighting, armed rural laborers, miners, and other civilians defeated Bolivia's army and brought the MNR to power. This was not simply another episode in Bolivia's long history of coups and counter-coups, most of them involving little bloodshed and few participants. About 600 people died in the fighting, and a large number of Bolivia's ordinary citizens were involved. For once, a revolution would make a difference in their lives.

Víctor Paz Estenssoro takes the presidential oath in 1952. AP/Wide World Photos

Immediately after returning to Bolivia and claiming the presidency, Paz Estenssoro formed a Ministry of Campesino Affairs to bring Indians into national affairs. *"Campesino"* referred to the same people as *"indio,"* but with the new word, the government hoped to improve the attitude toward the Indians. An act with much quicker results was the abolition of the requirement that voters know Spanish. Women also gained the right to vote, and in the next election, women and Indians swelled the electorate to five times what it had been in 1951.

The MNR, however, found it had released forces it could not fully control. Mine unions that had helped defeat the army demanded that the government immediately take over mines that belonged to the three largest private companies. They believed that this process, called "nationalization," would give the workers the wealth that had previously made a few individuals fabulously wealthy. In 1951 the MNR had promised to nationalize the three giant tin-mining companies. Pressure was so great that Paz Estenssoro had to come through only six months after taking office.

It was in the countryside, though, that real change was occurring. The civil war continued into 1953, beyond the control of the government. Armed rural laborers, organized into agricultural unions, had helped defeat the army. Now their goal was to claim the lands they had been working and drive away the *patróns* and their administrators. In many instances blood was shed, but for the most part it was a war of nerves. On the altiplano, for example, Indian *colonos* attacked the large flocks owned by the landowners, believing the *patróns* would abandon the *haciendas* if they became unprofitable. The laborers stole animals or killed them outright by mixing bits of barbed wire into their feed. The tactics were so successful that by the time the new government passed land reform legislation in 1953, the act only legalized what rural Bolivians had already achieved.

Successes of the Revolution

Rural Aymara and Quechua laborers became private farmers with a significant voice in government. The former *colonos* had no trouble taking control of the separate plots they had worked because they already lived on them. Though it took time for the government to give them legal ownership, their right to the land was never challenged.

Various arrangements were made concerning the larger lands that had been worked for the old landowners. The former *patróns* kept legal title to some of this territory, and in many cases they contracted with individual farmers or the agricultural unions to have the land worked. A minimum-wage law was passed to protect farmers who worked lands they did not own. Most important, the minimum wage was actually paid. Furthermore, the oppressive services once owed to the *patróns* were a thing of the past. Indians had more time to grow crops for their own purposes and to take part in community affairs—from traditional Indian festivals to local government.

The MNR government called for the formal education for all Bolivian children. Rural schools appeared all over the country, and some were even set up in the rooms of grand *hacienda* houses. For the first time the majority of Indian children began getting at least a few years of classroom education.

As part of its efforts to bring all Bolivians into national affairs, the MNR also took important steps to open up the eastern lowlands, particularly the Santa Cruz area. A paved highway from Cochabamba to Santa Cruz was completed in 1953. With the help of Argentina and Brazil, railroads from Santa Cruz connected with the rail systems of those countries. Thereafter, goods from Santa Cruz could more easily reach markets in the highlands, and products from the altiplano and *yungas* could easily reach markets in Argentina and Brazil.

Santa Cruz changed dramatically. Its population had been 42,000 in 1950. By 1960 it had passed Potosí, Oruro, and Cochabamba to become Bolivia's second largest city. In 1985 its population had reached 441,000, and most of Bolivia's agricultural exports came from the surrounding farmlands.

The subsoil wealth of the lowlands, oil and natural gas, had attracted attention early enough to be an issue in the Chaco War, and Bolivia formed a national oil company just after the war. It was after the revolution, however, that the country began to make significant use of the resources. By the mid-1980's, natural gas had overtaken tin as the nation's largest mineral export.

The major achievements of the 1950's—integration of the Indians into national affairs, extension of voting rights, land reform, education reform, and the opening of the lowlands—were permanent. For a time after 1952 there was fear that the former *patróns* might attempt to reestablish the *hacienda* system. This made rural farmers strong supporters of the MNR, and they helped the party stay in power for twelve years. But when the MNR was finally overthrown by the revitalized military in 1964, the reforms were too well established to challenge. In fact, the new military dictator, René Barrientos, immediately announced that he *supported* the achievements of the revolution. He claimed that the MNR had been deposed because it had become too corrupt to follow its own principles. No government since has tried to undo what was accomplished by the revolution.

Limits of the Revolution

Modern skyscrapers now tower above La Paz, but Bolivia remains a poor country. Infant mortality has been substantially reduced, but one baby in eight still dies before reaching the age of one. So far, Bolivia

Expanded educational opportunities, like this adult reading class, came with the reforms begun in 1952.   UNICEF/Ray Witlin

has not used its substantial resources effectively, and there is no better example than the Bolivian people themselves. About half of the work force is directly involved in agriculture, and yet Bolivia has often had to import more food than it exports to support its growing population. On the altiplano and *yungas*, farming methods have not advanced much beyond the traditional means used by the laborers during *hacienda* days.

Life in other sectors also remains difficult. World demand for tin fell sharply during the early 1980's, making it impossible to improve conditions for miners. Strikes and occasional violence have taken their toll, and miners still suffer from accidents and lung ailments. In many cases, they occupy the same houses they used in the time of Patiño. These are less crowded now, but only because fewer people can find work in the mines. In 1985 and 1986 the government closed some mines and attempted to make others more efficient. Tens of thousands of miners lost their jobs, and programs to provide for them were ineffective.

Between 1964 and 1982 Bolivia endured a period of almost uninterupted military rule. Some rulers endured for years, but at other times, coups brought in one dictator after another. Their policies and philosophies fluctuated widely.

Bolivia's economic state has been just as unstable. Extreme inflation (increasing prices for products and services) during the 1950's destroyed the boliviano, the basic monetary unit since the nineteenth century. When prices settled down, Bolivians exchanged a thousand nearly worthless bolivianos for each new peso. A generation later, in 1985, Bolivia suffered the world's highest inflation—11,750 percent. The currency was destroyed again, and this time Bolivians exchanged *one million* pesos for another new unit of currency, again called the boliviano.

A relatively healthy economy in the late 1960's and 1970's improved the standard of living for many Bolivians. However, much of the improvement was lost during severe economic hardship from 1982 to 1986. Mining output dropped and widespread flooding destroyed crops and livestock. Foreign loans to the government left Bolivia with a huge

debt without bringing expected development. A day's wage in 1983 purchased only two thirds what it had in 1978.

Historian James Malloy has called Bolivia's experience "The Uncompleted Revolution." His characterization will remain accurate at least into the 1990's. Bolivians have yet to achieve a fully unified nation benefiting from all the elements of their diverse heritage and rich land. Nonetheless, the country has come a long way since the days of the *patróns.*

Prices rose so quickly during the mid-1980's that the government printed money in increasingly large denominations for everyday use. When prices settled, a new currency was issued. The new 10-boliviano note (bottom) is worth the same as the old 10-million-peso note above it. David Nelson Blair

An Evolving People

There is no typical Bolivian.

A striking thing about a busy street scene in La Paz today is that one person can be so different from the next. Distinctive *chola* attire is common. A woman so dressed wears a long skirt, very wide over her hips because of its many layers. Her shoulders are wrapped in a colorful shawl that can be used for carrying anything from groceries to a baby. A small bowler hat sits on her head at a slight angle. Yet it is just as natural to see a person in clothes that would draw no special attention in any city across the Americas. A man may be dressed in factory-made trousers, a V-neck sweater, and a white shirt with open collar. Not only can this man and woman be found on the same street; they may be husband and wife walking arm in arm.

Just as dress varies widely in modern Bolivia, so do language, wealth, customs, race, and beliefs. Individuals express their identities through all these things, and the rich variety of sounds and sights in Bolivia reveals the great diversity of its people.

Three Tongues

Dozens of languages and dialects are spoken in Bolivia. Many are native tongues used by isolated Indians who still have little contact with the rest of the nation. The Mojo of the lowlands speak their own language, one of several Arawakan tongues used in Bolivia. More than a dozen distinct languages from the Panoan, Tacauan, and Guaranian families are spoken in remote areas of the east. The Uru of the southern altiplano have preserved their own language. Other languages have come with immigrants—among them English, German, Italian, and Japanese. Yet the vast majority of Bolivians speak the three languages that have dominated the region since the sixteenth century—Spanish, Quechua, and Aymara.

Spanish is the nation's official language. Legal documents, government records, and road signs use it. It is heard in all major cities and is the language of Bolivian business offices and television broadcasts. In cities and towns in the east, almost everyone speaks it. Spanish is called a Romance language because it is descended from Latin. As such, it is related to languages such as French, Italian, Portuguese, and Romanian. Spain's past empire made Spanish a world language, and nearly 300 million people speak it today. It is one of the official languages of the United Nations.

A Bolivian can understand Spanish speakers in Madrid or Manila or Miami, but the language is not the same everywhere. Latin American speakers pronounce some letters differently than Spaniards. Bolivians, in turn, speak less rapidly than most Latin Americans and do not drop syllables as frequently as some do. And, of course, Bolivian Spanish includes many words and phrases borrowed from the tongues of the Andes.

Of the hundreds of native languages in South America, more people today speak Quechua than any other. About 7 million people from southern Colombia to northern Argentina use it. Not surprisingly, this area roughly matches the old empire of the Quechua-speaking Incas. In Bolivia it is especially common in the montaña and in the southern altiplano around Oruro and Potosí. Some radio stations broadcast in Quechua. The language has a musical rhythm and smooth sounds that make it pleasant to hear. It is a good language for poetry.

In Aymara, words have harsher sounds. More than a million people use it today, though its speakers are not spread out as much as Quechua

A radio announcer wears a traditional chullo. *The airwaves in Bolivia carry broadcasts in Spanish, Quechua, and Aymara.*   Caroline Penn

speakers. Aymara is used in Peru and a little in northern Chile, but two thirds of all its speakers are Bolivians. Most live along the northern altiplano in the region around Lake Titicaca and La Paz. Some radio stations in the area broadcast in Aymara.

In both Quechua and Aymara, phrases are accented and words are compounded in similar ways. Scholars who study the origins of language believe they are related, and together they make up the Quechumaran language group. Yet a person who speaks only one cannot understand someone speaking the other. Individual words are too different in most cases:

	QUECHUA	AYMARA
one	uj	maya
two	iskay	paya
house	wasi	uta
water	yaku	uma
fox	atoj	tiwula
mountain	orgo	kollu

Still, the two languages, which began to mix even before the Inca conquest of the Aymara kingdoms, share many words, such as *oca* (a small sweet potato). Other words are similar. Three is *kinsa* in Quechua and *quimsa* in Aymara. In colonial and modern times, all three of Bolivia's major tongues have changed one another, and sometimes other languages as well. When the Spaniards first came to South America, Quechua speakers had long known about a large, graceful cat that in those days hunted in the Andes. Naturally they had a word for it. But the Spanish did not, since that particular species did not live in Europe. So the newcomers learned the native word, and before long it entered the Spanish language. Eventually *puma* even became a familiar part of English.

How Bolivian Languages Blend

Aymara, Quechua, and Spanish have influenced one another since the days of the Inca and Spanish conquests. Often one language simply picks up words from another. These terms are understood by virtually all Bolivians:

from Aymara   sorojche (altitude sickness)
              kantuta (national flower)
              Chuquisaca, Achacachi (place names)
from Quechua llama
              charango (stringed instrument)
              Oruro, Potosí (place names)
from Spanish pollo (chicken)
              san, santo, santa (saint)
              La Paz, Trinidad (place names)

Other words have changed slightly as they moved from one language to another. Here are Quechua words (left) that take a slightly different form in Spanish (and English):

kúntur → cóndor
wikuña → vicuña

Mixture occurs in another way when phrases are based on words from more than one language. These are phrases that mix Quechua

---

In the gradual change of language patterns, Spanish has a great advantage. News, literature, medical and other scientific articles, and educational materials of all kinds are all available in Spanish. Relatively little is written or translated into Aymara or Quechua. Any person who

(the first word) and Spanish (the rest):

chunku paloma (sweetheart)
sajta de pollo (a spicy chicken dish)

Sometimes the forms of one language mix with the words of another. In Spanish a suffix turns "bread" into "bakery":

pan → panadería

In Quechua "chicha" is a type of barley and corn beer. By adding the Spanish suffix, a new word is formed that means "tavern" in both languages:

chicha → chichería

The same thing can happen with names. Bolivian surnames may come from any of the major languages:

Chinapiri, Caranavi (Aymara)
Chungara, Cuíco, Mamani (Quechua)
Barrios, Velasquez (Spanish)

Almost all Bolivians receive Spanish given names. But Aymara and Quechua surnames are frequently added using overall Spanish construction. One author listed in "Suggestions for Further Reading" at the back of this book is Domitila Barrios de Chungara. "Chungara" is Quechua. The rest is Spanish.

desires a full education will have to learn a world language, and in Bolivia that usually means Spanish.

Today when Bolivian children first learn to speak, more learn Quechua than Spanish or Aymara. But many Quechua and Aymara speakers are learning Spanish as a second language, and now a majority of Bolivians can speak it. Perhaps a hundred years from now few will use Quechua or Aymara. Nevertheless, the influence of these important native Andean languages will certainly survive.

Ethnic Bolivia

The Bolivian people are as varied in their look as in their language. Women in particular wear distinctive clothing. The wide skirt, shawl, and bowler hat described at the beginning of this chapter are most common around La Paz. In and around Oruro, women wear stovepipe hats. Across the highlands, native dress, and especially headwear, varies so much that a knowledgeable person can tell a woman's region of origin by the clothes she wears. Men are less inclined to wear regional clothing, especially in big cities. Yet in the town of Tarabuco, men wear leather caps shaped like the helmets of Spanish soldiers and adorned with colored tassels and beads. The *chullo* is familiar over a wider area. This woolen cap with pointed earflaps has been traditional male headwear since before the arrival of the Spanish.

Other Bolivians, both men and women, prefer typically western clothes that can be found across the hemisphere. These range from jeans and leather jackets to neatly cut office suits for both sexes.

Race varies along the same lines as language. In the altiplano and montaña, most people can claim descent from the ancient Aymara and Quechua realms. Nationwide, just over half the people are predominantly Indian. Only one other country, Guatemala, has an American

Shoppers in a Tarabuco market wear a variety of modern and traditional clothing. The man with folded arms is wearing a leather cap shaped like a Spanish helmet. Hutchison Library/Bernard Régent

Indian majority. These people identify themselves as *campesinos* (males or mixed groups) or *campesinas* (females). Their hair is jet black and their skin is dark brown. In the highlands, the faces of adults in their thirties and beyond are usually heavily lined because of long exposure to the harsh sunlight of high altitudes. A far smaller percentage of the population in the lowlands is Indian. Nonetheless, Indians are joining the migration to the east.

Nearly a third of Bolivians identify themselves as *cholos* or *cholas*. They have a mixture of Indian and European blood, and they mostly live in the altiplano and montaña. (There is no longer the distinction between *cholos* and *mestizos* that there was in colonial days. *Mestizo* is a term still used throughout Latin America to refer to people of mixed Indian and European blood, but today Bolivian *mestizos* and *cholos* are the same people.)

Most of the remaining sixth of the population are people who identify themselves as *blancos* or *blancas*—literally "whites." They are predominant in the lowlands and also common in highland cities. Most are Hispanic, the descendants of the Spaniards and creoles of colonial times. They are lighter skinned, with hair usually ranging from medium brown to black. A few are descended from European ancestors other than Spaniards.

Finally, there are smaller minorities. Newcomers are now diversifying Bolivia's ethnic makeup, especially in the lowlands. The government has encouraged immigration; and Asians, particularly Japanese, are common around Santa Cruz.

As in colonial times, racial identity depends on much more than bloodlines. Language, education, dress, and wealth also make a difference. The usage of terms also varies, and they can become confusing. For example, throughout Latin America *"campesinos"* refers to farmers. In Bolivia it can also mean Indians in general or poorer country people (who happen to be mostly Indians). But wealthier white landowners who happen to live in the country are never called *campesinos.* In rural areas, many men still wear rough trousers, shirts, and coats made of home-made wool. They may speak only Aymara or Quechua and wear *abracas*, sandals made from tire tread and leather straps. Such people would be considered *campesinos*, even those with a little European blood.

A woman thinking of herself as a *chola* might be racially identical to another who sees herself as a *campesina.* She might derive her status from the fact that she can speak Spanish or that she is employed at a television station. Her clothes and shoes might be commercially made. Yet here again differences become vague. Most Aymara and Quechua women now have some commercially made clothes, and on trips to town they may be indistinguishable from *cholas.*

Even most whites from old Bolivian families have at least a trace of

These women are wearing the traditional chola *dress of the La Paz region, Bolivia's most familiar regional clothing style.* United Nations/Rothstein

Indian blood. Some have more than a little. These people may nonetheless be considered *blancos* because of their wealth. A Bolivian man who wears western suits, owns a business, and lives in a spacious, Spanish-style house will be accepted as a *blanco* even if he has visibly Indian features.

Clearly, social attitudes have not changed as quickly as legal status did following the revolution of 1952. Indians are often rural leaders and a few have been members of the national cabinet. Nonetheless, the great majority of leadership positions in government and industry belong to whites. Socially they are Bolivia's elite.

Social consciousness affects all Bolivians, but in many different ways. A woman moving to the cities will often learn Spanish and adopt *chola* or western dress as quickly as possible so she will not be stereotyped as a *monterosa*, which means "country hick." She will then be seen as a *devistida*, a woman who has left behind (or "divested" herself of) rural styles of dress and speech.

Stereotyping remains a problem. Longtime lowland residents are often alarmed by the appearance of *kollas*, Indian and *cholo* migrants from the highlands. (This term comes from Kollas, the name of an ancient Aymara kingdom.) Some whites continue to see Indians as lazy people who make no effort to improve the country and prefer to do only enough to just squeak by. Quechua and Aymara Indians beginning to learn Spanish may be written off as ignorant, or even stupid, because they have not mastered the grammar. The stigma can be so strong that some Indians are humiliated by their Aymara or Quechua surnames.

Yet attitudes are changing. Since the 1952 revolution, the government has tried to boost the Indian image by encouraging native folk festivals. More recently it has introduced Quechua as an elective course

Women around Potosí wear stovepipe hats.   Hutchison Library/Brian Moser

in the public schools. Aymara Indians have begun to shake off their old image of being suspicious, gloomy, and silent. Today some will say with pride, "I am Aymara."

A Changing Nation

Bolivia's population is changing in another way. Every day there are 560 more people in the country. As of 1990, there are about 7.4 million Bolivians, more than twice as many as at the time of the revolution. Scientists who study population trends believe that the country will continue to grow rapidly for generations to come. They expect a population of 9.7 million in 2000 and 18.3 million in 2025.

This growth, about 2.8 percent every year, is above the world average (1.8 percent) and far above the United States figure (1.0 percent). Because of such rapid growth and Bolivia's relatively short life expectancy, only a small minority of Bolivians alive today can remember the time of the *patróns*. Bolivia is a country of young people. Forty-three of every one hundred Bolivians are under the age of fifteen. (In the United States, only twenty-three of every one hundred people are that young.)

A young, quickly growing population faces many special problems. But young people are also quicker to learn new languages. They are more likely to start fresh in new places. Finally, they are more willing to accept the changing relationships among Bolivia's ethnic groups.

The movement taking place in Bolivia is obviously slower and less dramatic than that of the months following the 1952 revolution. Yet it is no less important. Growth, migration, immigration, shifting language patterns, and new feelings about ethnic identity are all social forces that are building on the achievements of the 1950's. Bolivia in the 1990's cannot help but be a changing country.

Young Bolivians gather at a video arcade in La Paz.   Caroline Penn

Paths of the Faithful

In 1582, according to Bolivian legend, an Indian carved a statue of the Virgin Mary holding her child high in front of her. He took it to a priest at Copacabana, an altiplano town on the shore of Lake Titicaca. The priest was dissatisfied because the figure's face was completely hidden by her uplifted arms. He put it aside and turned his attention elsewhere. When he looked back later, a miracle had occurred. The carved figured had lowered the child and revealed her face—an Indian face.

Beliefs, like language and bloodlines, have grown up from both European and native American roots. Oruro's Devil Dance and the Virgin of Copacabana show that the same is true of religion. A huge majority in Bolivia is Roman Catholic. Yet the nation's spiritual traditions come not just from Rome, but from the ancient Aymara kingdoms and the Inca empire.

The Roman Catholic Church

When Bolivia instituted Father's Day recently, it designated March 19 for the observance. That was considered the logical choice because it is the day honoring Saint Joseph, the stepfather of Jesus in Catholic tradition. The church's influence is visible across Bolivia. Thousands of the faithful parade through the streets of major cities on Good Friday and other traditional holy days. Twin bell towers rise above scores of churches, even in tiny towns. Enormous crowds greeted Pope John Paul II during his 1988 visit. For centuries the Roman Catholic Church has held enormous influence, and today ninety-five of every hundred Bolivians identify themselves as Catholic.

Catholicism has been the region's predominant religion since it arrived with the conquering Spaniards in the 1530's. It was the faith professed by Spanish monarchs for the centuries that they ruled Upper Peru. Early Bolivian presidents and dictators followed tradition, and through the nineteenth century Catholicism was the official religion of the nation. Church leaders and government leaders freely participated in one another's affairs.

In the early twentieth century, the relationship between the church and the government changed. Freedom of religion was established, meaning there would be no legal restrictions on other denominations. The government took control of education and required civil marriages. It no longer participated in church decisions.

Still, the church influenced national life and sometimes even clashed with the government. For example, a major principle of the 1952

This small church at Laja on the altiplano is more than three hundred years old.   David
Nelson Blair

revolution held that Bolivians should control their own country. Yet a
great majority of the priests in Bolivia were foreign-born, so MNR
leaders tended to distrust the church. Later, a dictator of the 1970's
arrested some Catholics because he thought their ideas about social
reform threatened his authority.

Recently church-government relations have improved. Church leaders have mediated strikes between the government and unions repre-
senting state miners, teachers, and bankers. Bolivian bishops have
spoken for the nation's poor at international economic conferences.
Pope John Paul II, speaking in Cochabamba, warned young Bolivians

to avoid seeking easy wealth through drug trafficking. The church is not the powerful force in national affairs that it once was, but it remains a visible participant.

Despite a huge Catholic majority, the church has limited contact with most people in Bolivia. Its most serious problem is the shortage of priests. Fewer than a thousand are active in the entire nation—less than one for every seven thousand Bolivian Catholics. As in earlier times, some of the smaller adobe churches in the countryside are visited by priests only once a year. Some remote towns never see them at all. Complicating the problem is the large proportion of foreign priests— more than two thirds of the nation's total. These have always faced the problem of mastering the Aymara and Quechua languages.

The sort of frustration faced by the church is illustrated by a situation that once developed in its seminaries. In the days when most Bolivian families could not send their children to schools, the seminaries were the only means to educate them. Many of the students, of course, were really interested in general education, not the priesthood. The seminaries ended up with a high dropout rate and the reputation that they catered to social climbers.

The Bolivian Flock

Even in areas where priests rarely appear, Catholic influence is highly visible, especially in the many festivals each year that are associated with church observances. Oruro's Devil Dance occurs just before Lent. Other annual festivals occur during Easter, the Holy Cross (May 3), Saint Peter's Day (June 29), the Nativity (September 8), and All Saints' Day (November 1). These are important social occasions, often giving families and friends the chance to visit and entertain. To some Bolivians, religion *is* nothing more than a series of social occasions. However, most Bolivians are very devout.

One example of this devotion is the active search for miracles. Near

Small but Reliable

In her novel *Bolivian Wedding* German writer Gudrun Pausewang examines a Bolivian style of Catholicism. Here villagers make a special effort to visit the grave of a thief who was wrongly accused of murder:

In the court records the guilt was still ascribed to Emilio, but no one believed it. Emilio was an innocent man who had been put to death, and therefore he was assured of God's special benevolence. His pleas were always heard. He interceded for people day and night. . . .

It was twenty-six years ago that he had been shot and now he, that brown-skinned Indio with the bushy eyebrows, sat with the white angels in paradise and looked out for the people of Marga-Marga, who had no other intercessor but him, apart from the Madonna of Copacabana. She was there for all of northwest Bolivia; her altars stood in every town and city as far south as Sorata. But Emilio belonged only to Marga-Marga, and maybe a little to the four other villages whose dead lay in this cemetery; five villages at the most—and you could take them all in at a glance. Here he knew every single person! It wouldn't be easy for him to forget anyone. With him one was well taken care of. He was only a small saint, but reliable.

From Gudrun Pausewang, *Bolivian Wedding* (New York: Alfred A. Knopf, 1971), p. 33.

Cochabamba is a rocky hillside called Urcupiña. Here, the faithful believe, the Virgin made another appearance. This belief draws tens of thousands of Bolivians to a three-day festival every August. Some bring toys—cars, trucks, houses, or even play money. They hope that the Virgin's influence will bring them the real item in the coming year. Others take stone chips from the hill, leaving stones from their own regions in exchange. They use the chips in the foundations of houses in the hope of bringing the Virgin's blessing to these new homes.

These practices may surprise Catholics who are accustomed to expressing their beliefs in other ways—through regular attendance at Mass, for example. But the festival at Urcupiña shows how much Bolivian Catholism has been affected by ancient American traditions. Ceremonies to bring blessings to new homes took place long before any Catholic priest came to the Andes.

This shrine honors the Virgin of Copacabana.   Ed Grazda

The Virgins of Copacabana and Urcupiña are only two of many in the country. Members of the armed forces look to the Virgin of Carmen. There is a Virgin of Cotoca near Santa Cruz and a Virgin of Guadelupe in Sucre. Many feel that these figures are all representations of the same person—the Virgin Mary, mother of Jesus. Yet beliefs vary. Some see each Virgin as a distinct person with a distinct character or personality of her own.

Sucre's Virgin of Guadelupe is covered with jewels and watches, gifts brought by the faithful to gain her favor. Hutchison Library/Brian Moser

Personality and personal appeals are important to Bolivians, which is one reason that the pope drew such huge crowds in this sparsely populated country. Many people placed special significance on touching him or even just seeing him. In the same way, they feel a personal prayer to a specific Virgin or saint is most likely to bring the blessing of that figure. Prayers may also be directed toward an *angelito* (little angel), the soul of a particular child who has died. A baptized child who dies before puberty is believed to be completely innocent and therefore to have special influence with God.

Many Bolivians feel that respect for spiritual beings is also important in avoiding misfortune. This is especially important to miners who face dangerous conditions daily. Working in deep shafts, they consider themselves to be in the realm of the devil. He is represented by Tío, whose name is the Spanish word for "uncle." A Tío figure waits just inside many mine entrances, and miners give him coca leaves and cigarettes so that they can work safely deep in his territory. They are careful not to mention the names of the saints for fear of antagonizing him. A few miners even refuse to work with picks. They are afraid that a tool in the shape of the cross will offend Tío.

Whether this is simply tradition or sincere belief depends on the individual. Many go along simply to follow custom and will say in private conversations that they don't take such practices seriously. Others are uncertain and feel it would be foolish not to make an effort to protect themselves. Still others are convinced that offerings to Tío appease him and prevent the catastrophes he would cause if he was displeased. In 1970 managers in one mine near Oruro tried to discourage regular offerings to Tío. But when an accident killed three young miners, some of their coworkers saw it as a sign of Tío's displeasure. They took a live llama into the mine and sacrificed it to appease him.

Tío sits at a mine entrance, where miners leave him offerings to ensure their safety in his realm. Hutchison Library/Brian Moser

Echoes of Ancient America

The mixture of Catholic and American religion was at times more of a clash. For example, when people fell ill or died, *karisirus* were often blamed. These were spirits that traveled at night and sucked the fat away from sleeping people. For a while after the Spanish conquest, Roman Catholic priests gained the reputation of being *karisirus*. Even into the twentieth century, some Indians feared priests.

Today other spirits continue to be taken seriously—*achachilas* of the mountains and lakes, *rayos* of lightning, *anchanchus* of evil places. When travelers see a new peak in the distance, they will stop, remove their hats, and make an offering of coca to its *achachila*. One of the most significant American figures is Pachamama. In Quechua her name means "earth mother," and she is particularly important at harvesttime. People attending an outdoor party may spill a little of the first drink onto the ground for Pachamama.

Aymara tradition also holds that each person has four or five souls and that one or more can leave the body for a time. Leaving one's home at night is sometimes discouraged because of the fear that loose souls can cause distress or illness.

The souls of children are particularly likely to stray. Thus parents fear taking a baby over a stream or lake because of the danger that its achachila will rob the baby of one of its souls. In one case, a boy fell into a river and became ill soon after. His mother believed that one of his souls had been lost. She took him back to the river's edge, whipped his cap against the riverbank, shouted his name, and had him eat a speck of dirt from the bank. He recovered, and she believed that she had called back the soul.

People may also connect human events with things that happen in nature. For example, pregnant women are advised not to handle hairy wool because of the fear it will result in an especially hairy child. They worry that winding yarn may cause a twisted umbilical cord or killing a snake may bring a child that cannot crawl. Abortion, because it is different from normal birth, is connected to hail, which is different from normal rain. Thus a woman who has aborted her child may be blamed if severe hail damages crops. On the other hand, a pregnant woman is encouraged to work in the field. Both her pregnancy and the fertility of the field are believed to benefit.

Rural people are the most likely to hold such beliefs, but migration has brought these Indian traditions into the cities to some extent. Almost all Bolivians are familiar with Ek'eko, the Aymara god of fertility and good luck. *Cholos* brought Ek'eko figurines to La Paz in colonial times, and now they have spread through most of the country. There are people from all ethnic groups who keep them at home for good luck, prosperity, and protection. An Ek'eko works like a charm bracelet. Each year or on special occasions something new is added to the load of belongings the Ek'eko carries.

Traditional Catholics dismiss Ek'eko and other native American beliefs as as superstition, while many rural people place great importance on those traditions, especially ones intended to keep away evil. However, there is not a sharp division between those who accept Catholicism and those who accept Indian beliefs. The same person might pray to the Christian God, Jesus, Mary, and the saints—but also to a *condormami*, the individual spirit of a house. Since the disposition of souls of the dead is important in both Catholic and Indian tradition, All Souls' Day (November 2) is a particularly important occasion in Bolivia. It is a time of visits to cemeteries and extensive prayers for the dead, particularly those who have died in recent years.

Aymara and Quechua Indians have kept their spiritual customs partly because priests are too few to closely control rituals. But there is a greater reason. These customs have endured also because they offer individuals satisfaction or comfort in a harsh world. They often bring extended families together. In rural areas, they provide activity during annual lulls, such as the time between planting and first weeding. Aging people no longer able to work will have the opportunity to preside over some ceremonies. This role allows them to maintain a feeling of usefulness and leadership in their final years.

Minority Beliefs

The last hundred years or so has brought new religions to Bolivia. In the 1880's, even before religious toleration was established in Bolivia, the American Bible Society sent missionaries into the country. They were followed by Canadian Baptists in 1898 and Methodists around the turn of the century. Today Baptists, Methodists, and Seventh-Day Adventists are all present. Immigrants from Asia are now exposing Bolivians to the traditions of Eastern religion.

Over the years, the Protestant denominations have been much more successful with educational and medical assistance programs than they have been in converting Bolivians to their beliefs. Nonetheless, with Bolivia experiencing a time of social change, many minor denominations have gained followings.

The future of religion in Bolivia is difficult to predict. Trends are much clearer in other areas—in language, for example. Yet change is inevitable in a society where a large percentage of the population is young and is being exposed to new customs, new languages, and new ideas. What does seem certain is that Bolivians will continue to draw on diverse sources in forming their spiritual beliefs.

A Nation's Character Through Art

Festivals in the tiny altiplano town of Compi honor saints and incorporate Indian beliefs. They provide people with a day to meet friends and members of their extended families. Local leaders get a chance to gain influence and prestige by paying for the costumed dancers, the brass band, and the folk musicians. People *expect* the town's political officeholders to do much of the providing.

The music and dance of the festivals are part of the religious, family, and political life of Compi. And across the nation, the arts and the lives of Bolivians influence one another. Architecture is wedded to religion through beautiful colonial cathedrals. Paintings, sculptures, novels, short stories, and poems are inseparable from the dreams and frustrations of Bolivia's changing society. All the arts mirror the special Hispanic and Indian character of the nation.

Architecture's Colonial Legacy

The church of San Lázaro in Sucre is as old as Spanish rule. It was built in 1538, the year Spaniards founded the city. Its silver altar panels and cedar confessionals are centuries old. Nearby, a larger cathedral built in 1559 holds the Virgin of Guadelupe and her treasures. Also within its walls are valuable religious paintings and a tabernacle of detailed silverwork.

Bolivia (Sucre in particular) is rich with beautiful colonial cathedrals. Architecture is a reminder that the nation was once a colony built on the wealth from early silver strikes. Buildings follow the basic lines that are common in Spain and elsewhere in Latin America. On the largest scale, cities and towns are built around central plazas, a layout of Arab origin that became popular in Spain while it was under Moorish domination.

Sucre is built around its Plaza 25 de Mayo, named for the date in 1809 when creole authorities first sought independence. From that square visitors can see neatly whitewashed walls and red-tiled roofs. Wrought-iron grillwork forms balconies and gates in the walls that often surround buildings. Columns and full Spanish arches appear everywhere.

La Paz has its Plaza de San Francisco, laid out in the shadow of its huge cathedral. Nearby the National Museum of Art is itself a work of art. Layers of columns and arches surround its central courtyard and fountain. The city's narrow side streets are lined with colonial mansions. Potosí has similar narrow streets, winding and paved with cobblestone.

Santa Cruz differs in one sense. It is laid out with twentieth-century roadways that follow concentric circles. Yet at the center of these beltways is an old Spanish plaza. Spanish form is not limited to the large cities. Countless tiny towns are built around plazas. Their small churches invariably include the characteristic twin bell towers of Spanish architecture.

Many of Bolivia's colonial buildings incorporate a style called "baroque." This uses much ornamentation and elaborate detail. It was popular throughout Spain and Spanish America, particularly in the seventeenth century. The baroque style allowed Upper Peru's builders to express their own traditions. Indian and *cholo* craftsmen usually produced the fine details in the silver, wood, and stone that went into the buildings. The faces they created were often Indian faces. Carved leaves, fruits, and birds were American leaves, fruits, and birds. From a distance, Bolivia's colonial buildings are Spanish. From an arm's length, they are distinctly Indian.

The Cathedral of San Francisco was begun in 1548. Its baroque details reveal the style of cholo *and Indian craftsmen.*   Both photos Doranne Jacobson

The Arts and Bolivian Life

Architecture had declined by the time Bolivia became a nation. The poverty and political chaos of the early republic prevented progress in this large-scale art form. The development of a local style ended, though naturally building continued. Sucre's Government Palace of the nineteenth century and the cathedral in Santa Cruz of the early twentieth are beautiful examples of more recent buildings. Yet these follow the earlier styles, and the modern skyscrapers of La Paz do not stand out from the skyscrapers typical in cities worldwide. The special character of modern Bolivia is better seen through paintings, sculptures, poems, plays, short stories, and novels.

Painting and sculpture had practitioners in colonial times. Jusepe Pastorelo worked at both during the first half of the seventeenth century. Melcher Pérez de Holguín became one of Spanish America's most outstanding painters in the second half of that century. Their work and the work of other colonial artists almost always involved religious subjects. After independence, Bolivian painters sometimes produced portraits and historical scenes, but the subjects they chose remained very limited for generations.

Colonial literature was even more constrained. It consisted mainly of hand-written chronicles such as descriptions of Potosí by Bartolomé Arzáns de Orsúa y Vela. Padré José de Acosta wrote a history of the Indians, and other Catholic churchmen wrote Aymara and Quechua dictionaries and grammar books. Little else was written because Upper Peru's Spaniards, creoles, and Indians were mostly illiterate. No publishing occurred because the first printing press did not reach the region until almost the time of independence. Arzáns' work, written in the eighteenth century, was not printed in quantity until the 1960's!

The Upper Peruvians did enjoy a little drama. The Indians memorized plays (since they had no writing) even before the Spanish came. Later, Arzáns mentioned that plays took place in Potosí. Unfortunately, almost nothing is known about Spanish or Indian drama of these times. Very little poetry was written. Juan Wallparrimachi Sawaraura wrote romantic poems in Quechua in the final colonial years, but he died at age twenty-one during the Wars of Independence.

During early nationhood, José María Dalence described Bolivian society and economics so skillfully that he is considered an early social scientist. However, works like his were rare, and virtually no fiction was written until late in the nineteenth century.

A woman weaver near Lake Titicaca.   United Nations Photo 155236 by John Isaac

Dalence, however, was more than a writer. He was an important Bolivian statesman and the man responsible for the nation's first census in 1846. This connection between literature and government was to expand quickly. In the 1850's, for example, some plays offended government officials, who stopped the performances.

From the 1880's through the 1920's, this connection came alive in much more constructive ways. Throughout Latin America, the arts began to examine themes from politics and national life, and Bolivia contributed to this movement. For a time political oratory was even considered an art form. Jaime Mendoza and Franz Tamayo wrote about the difficult lives of miners and Indians. Adolfo Costa du Rels described early-twentieth-century Bolivia. Poet Adela Zamudio described the exploitation of women. Many Latin American poets became highly respected worldwide for the first time, and the Bolivian Ricardo Jaimes Freyre was among them.

In 1926 the National Academy of Fine Arts was founded, and painters and sculptors began to work with national themes as writers had done earlier. A new generation of young artists began to work with watercolors, woodcuts, etchings, and prints—not just the oils that limited earlier artists. Some learned new techniques abroad, but returned to Bolivia and applied them to national and Indian themes. They portrayed local landscapes and customs. An outstanding example in recent decades is the work of sculptor Marina Núñez del Prado. She often worked in stone, from black granite to white onyx, and produced abstract Indian forms.

The shock of the Chaco War in the 1930's inspired a new type of novel. Augusto Céspedes wrote *Mestizo Blood*, which was extremely critical of the Chaco War governments. Many novels like it explored the brutal exploitation of Indian soldiers during the war. Other writers, like José Fellman Velarde, explored the exploitation of the Indian.

A rural craftsman shapes pottery.   United Nations Photo 155221 by John Isaac

It is no surprise that writers took up highly political themes, because they themselves were very political people. Mendoza was an important statesman. Tamayo was elected president (though a coup prevented him from taking office). Zamudio fought for women's rights, and Céspedes was a prominent member of the MNR. Modern Latin American writers and politicians are often the same people, and Bolivians follow that pattern.

But more than politics affected this writing in Bolivia. Writers, like other artists, began taking a pride in their country. They made an effort to show things that were unique to Bolivia, and much of their attention focused on its Indian heritage. Many of their countrymen have never shared this feeling, but it continues to be strong among the young.

This pride led to new studies and understanding. With rare exceptions, Bolivian writers have been whites working in Spanish. Yet there is a form of literature that came directly from ancient America—folktales. Indian folk art had long been known, especially in the form of finely woven wool garments and blankets. But following the revolution, writers explored Indian legends, stories, and fables. These studies helped them understand the lives the Indians had lived earlier. In 1980, Guillermo Francovich examined the entire course of Bolivian history through its myths.

Aymara folktales, for example, portray a world full of danger and deception. Souls are kidnaped; spells and counterspells are cast. Suspicion is deep, and trickster tales are common. In one story, a sparrow and a mouse agree to store food in the mouse's burrow. But the mouse tricks the sparrow and eats everything. The striped heads of some mice supposedly came from the resulting fight, but the real lesson is learned by the sparrow: Watch out for deceivers.

Tricksters may appear as foxes, skunks, condors, or hummingbirds. Significantly, one of the most popular tricksters is a human character. Pedro Ortemala always gets something for nothing and is never caught. His mischief says a great deal about the Indians' feeling that they are the victims of injustice.

The People's Beat

Music and dance are popular among Bolivians of all backgrounds. The country has produced some fine classical musicians, such as concert pianist Raúl Barrigan and the world-renowned violinist Jaime Laredo. Some composers have experimented with blending folk themes into classical compositions. But Bolivian music and dance are richest at folk festivals from the Cochabamba Valley to the altiplano, at carnivals in town plazas, in folk music clubs called peñas, and even on the patios of private homes. Like the other arts, most music and dance are centered on the things that are important to Bolivians—religion, folk tradition, and everyday events like courting.

Musicians are traditionally men among Aymara Indians, though women participate in singing. Until recently, most dancing was done by men. Especially in the last ten years, though, dancing in mixed groups has become much more common.

During the spring fertility rites in Compi, competing chains of dancers maneuver to the music, each trying to cut through the other's line. Throughout the highlands, individual dances are as unique to their regions as are the styles of dress. The dances often involve elaborate

A La Paz group plays Andean music on traditional instruments.   Doranne Jacobson

An altiplano couple dances at a community festival celebrating the opening of a facility to clean sheep. Caroline Penn/Foster Parents Plan

costumes, many stemming from Indian tradition. Such customs draw community people into dance and ceremony.

Spanish customs also get people involved. Sucre, Oruro—many Bolivian communities—practice the *retreta.* After church, townspeople gather in the plaza, and the teenagers begin circling. The girls move in one direction, the boys in the other, and everyone gets a look and a chance to meet everyone else. Fathers and mothers settle on the benches and keep an eye on everything that goes on.

Santa Cruz practiced the traditional *retreta* well into the 1970's, but it took on a new form as the automobile became increasingly common. The girls now take Sunday-night strolls by twos and threes along a wide avenue in the Equipetrol neighborhood of the city. The boys go by in cars. The new style and location doesn't alter the traditional purpose of the ceremony. Lots of boys meet lots of girls.

Romance is the theme of much Bolivian music, and soft, romantic music is especially popular in Santa Cruz. A young man with a guitar can often be seen playing in the tropical garden patio of his girlfriend's house. In fact, to win her family's favor, he won't hesitate to serenade her mother on the older woman's birthday.

The traditional Spanish guitar is an example of Bolivia's European heritage. The *cueca* dance, full of hand clapping and waving handkerchiefs, also has Spanish roots. But Indian influence is also deep. An

Flute players perform in a Copacabana festival.   Ed Grazda

instrument called the *zampoña* consists of lengths of cane tightly bound in a line—an American version of panpipes. Notched flutes are also made of cane. A popular type 9 or 10 inches long (23 to 25 centimeters) is called a *quena*. A smaller version popular with young boys is called a *pinquillo.*

It is no surprise that music has brought Spanish and Indian influences together. The *charango* is a stringed instrument that developed from both cultures in Spanish America. Baroque carvings as early as the eighteenth century show it clearly, and mule traders spread it over a wide area. Today it is popular in Bolivia, Argentina, and Peru. The *charango*'s small body may be made of wood, but often it is the shell of an armadillo. It is strummed like a guitar, but its range is higher, and it usually has five pairs of strings.

The *charango* is part of Bolivian life. It is traditionally a man's instrument used in courting. But it can also accompany singing and dancing at family parties. And it is a festival instrument. In the open country it has another purpose. A rural man who has to travel some distance on foot often strums his *charango* as he walks along. This is an old tradition. Ages before the car radio, traveling music was part of Bolivian life.

Daily Life

A family patio is little more than a ledge in Villa Fatima, a community built on the steep canyon wall overlooking La Paz. A waist-high wall of rough bricks on the downhill side keeps small children from tumbling into the lot below. Another side of the patio is open, giving the family access to a stone staircase that serves as a community alleyway.

Elsewhere, a very different family patio may include deck chairs, a grill, and even a large swimming pool sunk into the yard. If such a house is in Santa Cruz, its location is revealed only by the tropical butterflies fluttering about the colorful garden. The dust and the traffic of the city are hidden by the high stone wall that completely surrounds the family enclave.

A Bolivian's day-to-day life naturally depends on his or her wealth,

La Paz's Villa Fatima neighborhood is built on the canyon walls overlooking the central city. David Nelson Blair

A well-to-do home in Santa Cruz's Equipetrol neighborhood.   David Nelson Blair

but that is only one of many things that affect the way each person lives. A city dweller finds a greater variety of entertainment than a country dweller. A miner faces different problems from those of a farmer. Just as there is no typical Bolivian, there is no typical lifestyle.

Home and Community

The dark, primitive huts that were once the rule for rural laborers are becoming a thing of the past in Bolivia. Yet for most Bolivian families, housing remains very basic. Because wood is not abundant near most of the population, rural homes are usually made of adobe brick and corrugated tin roofs. Some have just a room or two; others may include a second floor.

A home in the country might have an open court for a kitchen. Typically it will include a clay stove, clay or metal pots, and a few metal utensils. Beds, a table or two, and a few straight chairs furnish the rest of the house. Transistor radios reached the rural population years ago, and now many families also own bicycles.

As in much of Latin America, families eat the several varieties of home-grown potatoes and grains. They cook *lawa*, a tasty soup made by grinding corn and stirring it into water. Corn, a major staple, is also crushed, boiled, and allowed to ferment into *chica*—corn beer. Diet has become more varied in recent decades, however. Many rural families now routinely purchase items like bread, noodles, sugar, rice, and coffee at town markets.

Early on, children growing up in rural areas begin helping with chores—carrying water, cooking, and caring for younger brothers and sisters. Boys and girls spend many hours herding. Four- and five-year-olds start out under the supervision of parents or older children. But by the time they are eight, they may be in charge of pigs on their own. As they learn responsibility, they will be trusted with sheep. Finally, around age ten, they will look after the most valuable animals, such as cows or llamas. When children are herding in groups, they often spend hours playing tag and similar games.

Rural homes are usually very isolated. A weekly visit to a town store or a trip to see cousins is a major event in a child's routine. But most children do attend schools in the scattered small towns. There they copy civics or arithmetic lessons from blackboards and have the chance to

This woman raises chickens on the altiplano. Caroline Penn/Foster Parents Plan

Recipes

Staples such as potatoes, corn, and chicken are common ingredients in Bolivian recipes. Here are three:

Lawa de Choclo (A cream of corn soup that serves six)
> *8 ears of corn*
> *8 cups clear broth*
> *6 slices soft white cheese*
> *Finely chopped parsley to taste*
> *Salt to taste*

Cut raw corn from ears. Blend in an electric blender with 1 cup warm broth. Bring remaining broth to a rapid boil in large saucepan. Add corn mixture, stirring gently. Reduce to medium heat for approximately 15 minutes. Serve in bowls over cheese slices. Sprinkle with parsley and salt to taste.

Picante de Pollo (A spicy hot chicken dish that serves six)
> *Broth*
> *1 chicken (4 to 5 pounds) cut into 6 sections*
> *Dried hot ground red peppers to taste*
> *1 cup chopped onion*
> *1 cup peeled, chopped tomatoes*
> *1 cup green peas*

play a little soccer. Growing up involves many landmarks. The Aymara, for example, have a special ceremony for a child's first haircut. A young man often graduates to adulthood by entering military service, a young woman when she marries.

½ teaspoon ground cumin

1 teaspoon oregano, crumbled

3 cloves garlic, finely chopped

3 cups chicken broth

2 tablespoons oil

Other ingredients

6 boiled potatoes

1 finely sliced onion

1 chopped tomato

½ cup chopped parsley

Mix broth ingredients in medium saucepan. Bring to a rapid boil over high heat. Reduce heat and simmer covered for 1 hour or until chicken is tender. If mixture is drying out, add more broth or water to provide gravy. Serve on plates over potatoes. Add sliced onion and chopped tomato. Sprinkle with parsley.

Plato Paceño (An easy dish, meaning "La Paz Plate," that serves one)

1 ear of corn

1 potato, unpeeled

½ cup lima beans

3-ounce chunk lightly floured brick cheese

Boil corn, potato, and lima beans in separate saucepans. Heat cheese in greased frying pan until base browns and begins to melt, then turn over and repeat. Serve together on a large plate.

As they get older, rural children commonly become interested in anything they hear about cities. La Paz may seem a wonderland of automobiles, television, and daily street markets. Many children will eventually migrate to the city. From ancient times the great majority of

Bolivia's people had been country dwellers. But now about half live in cities and larger towns.

To a person used to an occasional rural market, the sights and even smells of city markets are fascinating. In plazas and along streets in La Paz, countless vendors sell goods from underneath plastic awnings they have erected for shade. For blocks, booth after booth offers brightly colored wool blankets and shawls, some folded in tall piles, others hanging fully displayed. Raw coca leaves are scooped directly from huge bags. Traditional *chullos* (men's knitted caps) and stacks of *chola* derbies are for sale.

Food is always available in the streets of Bolivian cities. *Chorizo* is a spicy sausage. An *empanada* is a cheese-filled pastry popular throughout Latin America. The *salteña* is especially popular in Bolivia. This is a highly spiced, crusty turnover filled with meat, potatoes, raisins, hard-boiled eggs, and olives. There are also supermarkets, where shoppers can load their carts and go through checkout counters. In many of these same stores, individual vendors set up stands and sell agricultural goods independently.

Housing in the city also offers advantages. Even communities where the homes consist of rough bricks and tin roofs often have electricity. The main room of a family house will be illuminated by a bulb hanging by its cord from the ceiling. Another advantage is that city children meet many more people outside their extended families. They usually have the opportunity to attend public schools nearer to their homes than rural children.

City life, however, has its dangers and disadvantages for the poorest Bolivians. In La Paz, for example, they are crowded onto whatever free space they can find. As the city's population has grown, many newcom-

On this altiplano farm a young girl tends the family sheep.   Caroline Penn

A La Paz vendor sells pots in an open market.   Doranne Jacobson

ers have built homes on the steep canyon slopes around the city. The unusually heavy rains in 1986 caused landslides that destroyed homes along the slopes and took lives.

Middle-class and wealthy Bolivians live far more comfortable, secure lives. They occupy larger, better-built apartments or houses. Following the style of most Latin American countries, these are virtually always surrounded by high walls. Outside lawns or grounds are unheard-of; the walls enclose the entire property including the carport or garage. Walls typically separate properties or reach all the way to sidewalks or streets.

Skyscrapers contrast with the mountains and high clouds in La Paz.   David Nelson Blair

The wealthiest Bolivians are those owning extensive property. They are a tiny minority, usually the descendants of a few influential families that ruled Bolivia in the past. Their homes in both cities and the country can be mansions with half a dozen spacious bedrooms, well-equipped modern kitchens, and abundant space for entertaining family and friends. These homes often include an apartment for live-in servants. A family might well have an expensive European car.

Professional people who earn salaries or make profits from small businesses make up Bolivia's middle class. This group barely existed before the twentieth century and still accounts for less than a tenth of the population. A middle-class house more typically resembles a U.S. middle-class home in size and layout. Television and other modern appliances are the rule. A servant responsible for cooking and cleaning might live in one room or might not live in the family's residence at all. The family car is an import from Asia, Europe, or the Americas.

Wealthy and middle-class families almost always send their children to private schools, many of them church affiliated. Some of these children will later attend Bolivia's universities. St. Francis Xavier University in Sucre was founded in 1624, making it one of the oldest in the Western Hemisphere. Any of Bolivia's major cities can provide a university education, though students of well-to-do families often study abroad.

Some things unite just about all Bolivians. One is soccer. True, some of the wealthiest Bolivians join foreign tourists on the ski slopes of Chacaltaya. Or they may hit long drives in the thin air of Malasilla, the world's highest eighteen-hole golf course. But Bolivia's best-known athletes are soccer players, and soccer is the uncontested favorite sport of the nation.

The well-off usually consider *chica* drinking and coca chewing to be crude. Yet they often enjoy *tojorí*, a drink that is thick, pulpy, and sweet.

Like *chica*, it is made from corn. And almost every wealthy or middle-class home stocks *mate de coca.* This extremely popular, respectable beverage is brewed and sipped like tea. It even comes in neat, commercially packaged tea bags. Yet inside are coca leaves.

The Role of Women

Bolivia observes Mother's Day on May 27. The day commemorates a battle during the Wars of Independence in which the women of Cochabamba successfully defended the city against Spanish forces. Women have repeatedly distinguished themselves in many ways. When miners by the thousands left for the Chaco War, women went into the shafts to carry on the labor. Others have made names for themselves in art and politics. A few women are practicing architects. In 1979, Lydia Gueiler Tejada became one of the first women to become president of a Latin American nation.

A few professional women, like this architect in La Paz, are taking on new roles in Bolivia.
United Nations/Jeffrey Fox

Nonetheless, women rarely have the opportunities that men do. Women's day-to-day routines vary a lot depending on their circumstances. A rural woman may spend hours at a time hand weaving a wool blanket on a crude frame, weeding a potato field with hand tools, or taking animals to pasture. An urban woman has greater opportunities and may work in an airport, hotel, restaurant, business or government office, or university. Yet most frequently, the activities of Bolivian women, especially married women, center on the home and family.

In this respect, Bolivia is similar to other Latin American nations. Catholic and Spanish traditions assign distinct roles to men and others to women. For centuries, custom has placed the husband at the head of the family. It has left the wife with responsibility for cooking, cleaning, and child care—chores the husband traditionally shuns.

Names say a lot about the place of women. A child of either sex will receive a double surname—the father's surname first, the mother's next. When a woman marries, she drops her mother's surname and adds her husband's following the word "de." This Spanish prefix means "belonging to." Latin American women are *not* legally the property of their fathers or husbands. Yet a Latin American woman who takes up a nontraditional role risks the scorn of her family or community.

In Bolivia, mine-industry jobs are a good example. Though the Chaco War era demonstrated that women could handle mine work, customs and the taboos kept them from continuing those jobs after the war. At best, a woman in a mining camp might find employment sorting through piles of discarded stone for the last traces of useful ore. Or she might bake *salteñas* to sell to miners and their families. She may leave the camps to help her relatives in the country during harvest. And if she becomes a widow, as so many mine wives do, she might have to return to the country permanently and depend on those relatives for support.

Since wealthy and middle-class Bolivians employ servants, domestic service is another source of employment for poor women. Still, the work follows traditional ideas about a woman's role. Most work as cooks or maids. Even if a couple is hired jointly into domestic service, the wife will almost always take on the cooking and cleaning. The husband, on the other hand, will attend to driving, gardening, and other outdoor jobs that are considered suitable for men.

The lack of opportunity begins early. In rural areas, parents may not see any value in an extensive classroom education for a girl. Despite laws that require eight years of school for every Bolivian child, many receive much less, and a girl is especially likely to get just a few years. As a result, nearly half of Bolivia's women are illiterate, whereas three quarters of its men can read. Some men insist that their wives stay away from alcohol. The reason: The husbands may want to drink excessively, and they expect their wives to get them home.

The fact that a woman works does not relieve her of family duties. Some centers now provide child care, but these are not available to most working mothers of small children. A mother in a rural field or a city market often carries a small child in her shawl. A domestic servant may bring her toddler to her employer's home.

The Workplace

In large mining camps the workday begins early, and a union siren wails at 5 A.M. to wake up the men. Younger men take the most strenuous positions as drillers and blasters. Older men operate winches or load and push carts of ore along narrow rails. Numerous support jobs keep the operation going as new shafts are dug and mined. Rail setters must run tracks deep into the mine. The mines need pipe fitters to put in plumbing, which drains water out of flooded shafts or provides water to keep men and machines cool. The wooden beams that prevent cave-

Women prepare to bake bread in an outdoor oven.   Carolyn Watson

ins require carpenters. Shift chiefs and group leaders supervise the operations.

The work is dangerous. A drill unexpectedly hitting hard rock may buck and injure the man operating it. Cave-ins are a constant threat. So is the gas that may take lives without warning. Dynamite, sometimes used to expose the last traces of ore, may accidentally detonate before miners are clear. Another serious danger is lung disease. Constant exposure to mine dust commonly leads to respiratory diseases for men who work in the mines for many years.

In this hostile environment, one man's carelessness might easily cause another man's death. For that reason, the miners place great value on teamwork and responsibility to one another. Miners call one another *ñaña,* a Quechua word for "brother."

Men working in the gas and oil industry in the east also face strenuous work—constructing and operating the heavy drilling equipment used to reach deposits far underground. This type of work isolates workers, since gas and oil reserves are often in the most remote areas of the country. A worker's life often consists of a succession of eight-week cycles—four weeks at a distant worksite, four weeks back with his home and family.

Agricultural labor also has its migrants. Not every Indian family owns its own land. Many landless altiplano residents regularly travel to the montaña and earn a wage working on plantations there. Those that do have land work with tools improved since the days of the *patróns*, but farming methods still rely on muscle power for the most part. Axes, hoes, and plows now use metal parts instead of wood, but farmworkers continue to plow, plant, weed, and harvest by hand. Workers often must walk long distances from their homes to their fields, and in most places the only wheel to be seen is on the hand-pushed wheelbarrow. Men and women often work together in agriculture. Typically men do the most strenuous work, handling a plow, for example. Women will do less laborious jobs, breaking up clumps of dirt or planting seeds. But for men and women alike, the work is long, hard, and tedious. Harvesting potatoes, for example, requires farmers to spend hours bent over digging the potatoes out of the ground by hand.

Improvement has come in transportation. Usually a group of workers will band together and hire a truck for transport. Truck ownership is still beyond the means of most, though a few have achieved it. Dependence on *cholo* middlemen is not as great as it once was. This new style of taking products to market has also increased the contact between the

Pedestrians and motorists pass the municipal building in La Paz, location of the mayor's office. Embassy of Bolivia

country and the city. Indians from the northern altiplano, for example, will often have friends and acquaintances in La Paz or Cochabamba. They are now more aware of what is happening throughout the nation. Women in particular make these contacts because they do most of the selling in the city markets.

In the cities, a man or woman might be employed in banking, government work, selling, or manufacturing. La Paz cab drivers shuttle air travelers between the airport and the city below. Journalists, printers, and technicians work on the nation's thirteen daily newspapers and nearly two hundred radio and television stations. In short, people engage in all the activities that keep urban centers and the nation running.

Coping

To a foreign traveler in the Bolivian highlands, coping means dealing with the extreme altitude. A person with heart or respiratory problems should not go there at all without consulting a doctor. Altitude is a well-known problem because it affects every foreigner who steps off a plane at El Alto (the name of this airport means "the high one"). But for the Bolivians, coping means more than enduring a thin atmosphere in some parts of the country. For rural parents, it can mean placing a girl of ten in change of an infant for a week at a time while they bring in a harvest. For a miner, it may mean going without a helmet, gloves, and iron-tipped boots so his family can save a little extra. He might even oppose expensive measures to protect health because they could force layoffs. Each Bolivian must find ways to get from one day to the next in often difficult circumstances.

The Altitude

Tourists are not the only victims of altitude. Internal combustion engines work at lower efficiency in the thin air. That means cars and trucks can't operate at full power. Water boils at a lower temperature at high altitude—instead of the familiar 212°F. (100°C.) at sea level, water boils at 182°F. (83°C.) at 10,000 feet (3,000 meters)—so car radiators are quick to boil over. Drivers on the altiplano, especially those in older vehicles, carry jugs of water along to be safe. Even meals are affected. Because of the lower boiling point, coffee and tea can never be served quite as hot. Cooking takes longer because moisture will boil away if high temperatures are used. It may be necessary to use a pressure cooker to hard-boil an egg!

Altitude's most serious effects are on people. This includes Bolivians themselves, since altitude varies so much within the country. Visitors from lowland Santa Cruz are in for trouble if they don't follow these precautions on their first day in highland La Paz or Oruro:

—Rest as much as possible. Avoid walking even a few blocks.

—Go slow during any walking or stair climbing that cannot be avoided (getting to a hotel room, for example).

—Avoid alcohol.

Violators are subject to *sorojche*, the highlands' notorious altitude sickness. This is no joke or legend. At sea level, barometric pressure is 29.9 inches (760 millimeters). On the altiplano, it averages 18.3 inches (465 millimeters). That means there is less oxygen in each breath. Muscles tire quickly, and mild exertion can leave a person panting. There's more: *Sorojche* can inflict a stinging headache and cause acute nausea. It completely incapacitates many travelers who aren't careful.

Physically, Bolivian highlanders are accustomed to the altitude because their ancestors have lived there for centuries. But they are prone to respiratory problems if they move to the lowlands, especially since a change in climate accompanies the change in altitude. Illness struck on a tragic scale when Indian soldiers left the highlands for the first time to fight in the Chaco War. The region's unfamiliar heat, relatively thick atmosphere, and tropical diseases killed thousands.

And in some ways, highlanders themselves can be adversely affected by high altitude. Lung diseases like pneumonia and the dust-related disorders that afflict miners are more likely to kill where oxygen is scarce. Heart problems may also be complicated by the altitude. One Bolivian woman born in highland Potosí later lived for many years in lowland areas. Eventually she developed a minor heart problem. Though this condition was unrelated to the change in altitude, it prevented her from ever returning to the region of her birth.

Family Support

Geography accounts for only a small number of the problems facing Bolivians. Like people everywhere, they want respectable food and shelter for themselves, opportunity for their children, and security for the aged. Individuals rely a great deal on the family for both physical and psychological support.

Bolivians of both Indian and Hispanic backgrounds have strong families to look to when times get difficult. Social security programs cover only about a quarter of the population, so families usually care for their elderly. Families also address much simpler problems, like the depression a woman often feels after giving birth. The Aymara have a ceremony called the *asuti* to deal with just that. A few days after a woman has given birth, teenage family members and friends put on a play in her honor. The actors get a chance to mock the adults present, and a lot of playful teasing goes on between the cast and the audience. The whole point is to cheer up the new mother.

Indian tradition calls for strong family relationships, and the Indian idea of the family extends beyond parents and children. It includes grandparents, aunts, uncles, and cousins. In markets, it is not uncommon to see related women taking turns holding a child. Some family relationships do not involve blood ties at all. *Compadrazgo* joins unrelated people of different generations. It is a relationship like that between godparent and godchild, and can be established at a marriage

Children play at a government day-care center near La Paz. However, most families do not have access to such facilities. UNICEF/Ray Witlin

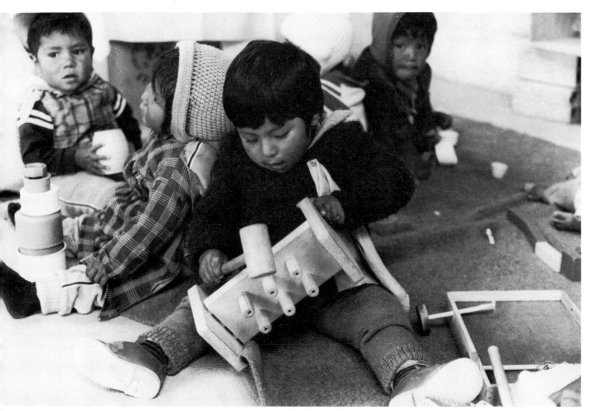

or a baptism. The care a family provides for its members might be as simple as a grandparent baby-sitting a child. Or it might be more complex; one Indian custom calls for family supervision of trial marriages that may last up to two years.

Families following Hispanic tradition are quite similar. Here, too, is the custom of assigning godparents called *padrinos* or *padrinas.* And the extended family remains very close with a strong sense of obligation among family members.

For example, if travelers have relatives in the area that they are visiting, it goes without saying that they are welcome in the relatives' home. Usually, they need only mention their travel plans, and they will get an invitation without asking for one. In fact, it is not unusual for a family member to arrive unannounced. The hosts feel an obligation to do whatever they can—not just for the relatives who have opened their homes in the past, but for any member of the extended family.

Family support can take all forms. Bolivians traveling abroad often carry shopping lists from other family members since certain items may be too expensive or not available at home. An uncle in a position of authority in business or government often feels obligated to help numerous nieces and nephews find jobs. This is so common a solution for families that it becomes a problem for government and business. Nonetheless, the Bolivian—like most Latin Americans—feels a pressing duty to family.

Solutions in a Poor Country

Money is a problem in Bolivia. This is especially true for the nation's many poor, but all Bolivians share difficulties unknown in countries with advanced economies.

Rapidly rising prices are a constant worry. Bolivians remember that twice in recent decades extreme inflation has caused their currency to become virtually worthless. During those times it was impossible to save money in the normal way. The money needed to buy four gallons of milk at the beginning of 1985 could not buy enough to fill a teacup a year later. Early in 1986 it was not uncommon for a person to carry 200 million Bolivian pesos at one time. A meal at a modest restaurant exceeded 12 million pesos per person.

Rich and poor alike have found a solution—the use of U.S. dollars. A person receiving bolivianos (the new currency) will change the money into dollars at the first chance. A domestic servant is as likely as a wealthy businessman to have savings in dollars. Only when it is time to spend it is the money converted back to bolivianos. Dollars are commonly accepted for purchases.

This money exchange is so common that a whole industry devoted to currency exchange has developed. It has nothing to do with official banks. In any urban center, there are hundreds of *cambistas*, people on the streets who change bolivianos to dollars and vice versa. The practice is technically illegal, but is almost universally accepted. In some places, like La Paz, it takes place discreetly. The *cambistas* can always be found along side streets but do not work openly on main thoroughfares. *Cambistas* may quietly visit the homes of their regular customers.

In other places, like Santa Cruz, *cambistas* will set up tables or booths along main streets. At times when their exchange rate is fluctuating rapidly, they may hold up placards—even small chalkboards—to advertise the rate of the moment. Authorities rarely interfere, and in recent years they have even alerted the *cambistas* to watch for counterfeit money discovered in circulation.

The boliviano has been relatively stable in recent years, but Bolivians do not see that as a sign that it will remain so. The practice of street-side currency change is still going strong.

Dollars and bolivianos are being exchanged during this casual curbside gathering in Santa Cruz. The seated man is a cambista *holding a pack of bills in his left hand.*
El Mundo/Editorial Oriente S.A.

A foreign dollar can ease the uncertainty of saving money in Bolivia, but for most things in day-to-day life there is no foreign substitute. Roads are an example. Anyone traveling the winding, treacherous roads of the montaña understands why ground travel in Bolivia can be difficult. On the altiplano, long stretches of the Pan American highway consist only of packed dirt and gravel. Even traveling within cities can be difficult. The major spokes and beltways of Santa Cruz's road system are paved, but most side streets are not. As the city grows, more and more motorists must maneuver through intersections and traffic circles—without the help of stoplights. One of the ways that Bolivians have coped with an inadequate road system is by developing air travel.

International airports serve La Paz and Santa Cruz. Other cities have municipal airports, and many landing strips make remote areas of the east accessible. Air travel is the preferred way, and sometimes the only way, to travel between regions.

Settling for Less

Only well-off families can send their children to study abroad, and most Bolivians cannot afford the private schools in the country. They must settle for public schools that have very limited resources. Poor communities often make do by putting schools in multipurpose buildings. Thus classes must compete with other community activities for time in the buildings. In rural areas, school might be held in a spacious but decaying room of an old *hacienda* house. Public-school teachers receive very low pay and usually are poorly trained. In trying to cope themselves, they will often strike for improved wages, leaving schools closed for weeks at a time. Most Bolivians are forced to learn as best they can under the circumstances.

All too often, they must accept a standard of living far below the norm in the western hemisphere. Poor children who want to play soccer sometimes inflate the gall bladder of a cow and use it for the ball. More troubling is the solution a rural mother uses when she is unable to give her child mother's milk. She cooks corn in water, and the child must settle for the resulting liquid. A more common problem involves the countless markets of the streets and plazas throughout the country. Fruits, vegetables, and meats are constantly exposed to the open air—a condition particularly hazardous in warm, lowland parts of the country. Moreover, most Bolivians do not have the means to freeze or refrigerate food. They must look to other, less satisfactory means of preventing spoilage. For example, meat can be preserved by salting and drying. The

When Coping Fails

In a mining camp in the mid-1950's, a motherless teenager tried to take her sisters to school with her. But the little girls disrupted class too much, and the teacher wouldn't let them stay. Domitila Barrios faced a dilemma. She could drop out or leave her young sisters unsupervised while she continued classes. Years later she described the tragic consequences of her decision:

Then my father told me to leave school, because I already knew how to read and I could learn other things by reading on my own. But I didn't obey him and I continued going to my classes.

Then one day the little one ate carbide ashes that were in the garbage pail, the carbide that's used to light the lamps. They'd thrown food on top of the ashes and my little sister, who I think was hungry, went to eat out of the can. She got a terrible intestinal infection and then she died. She was three years old.

I felt guilty about my little sister's death and I was very, very depressed. And even my father would say that it had happened because I hadn't wanted to stay home with the kids.

From Domitila Barrios de Chungara, *Let Me Speak!* (New York and London: Monthly Review Press, 1978), p. 54.

result is less healthy than refrigerated meat. Diet in general suffers because of all these practices. The average Bolivian consumes only 2,061 calories per day (56 percent of what the average American consumes).

Bolivians have often faced difficulty finding steady, productive livings. Unemployment became severe in the hard times of the 1980s.

Miners accept dangerous conditions in their daily work.   United Nations/Photo by Jerry
Frank

Many laid-off miners found social services inadequate, and some were forced to house their families in tents. The long-term growth of the population on the altiplano has meant that a smaller proportion can support themselves through agriculture. Many migrate to urban areas. These pressures have increased competition for jobs in the cities. For example, a bricklayer who can only find occasional work will have to depend partly on other family members, perhaps even very young ones.

Children learn to cope early in Bolivia. They may wait on tables in a family restaurant. Or they may do countless menial jobs to earn meager tips. Small boys will lug wheelbarrows full of groceries for market shoppers. Or they may try to sell cheap souvenirs to tourists. Sometimes a child will stand guard over a parked car for an hour or more while its driver takes in a show or tends to errands. The shoppers, tourists, or motorists may help these poor children to survive. But at the same time, collecting tips keeps these same children out of school. Bolivia requires all children between eight and fourteen to attend school, but only about three quarters in this age group actually do. A lack of education coupled with poor nutrition reduces a child's chance for a more prosperous life in the future.

Naturally, children growing up in these circumstances are often frantic to share in any prosperity they may see around them. This sort of desperation can lead to crime anywhere in the world, and Bolivia is no exception. There is good reason to hire a child to watch a car. Likewise, the walls around houses are not there just for privacy. It is common to see jagged fragments of glass cemented into the tops of the walls to keep out thieves. Many a woman's canvas handbag displays a stitched-up gash. Working as deftly as pickpockets, children in crowds cut open bags with razor blades and steal the contents.

At its worst, coping can be a struggle for life itself. Bolivia's health care has improved greatly in recent decades. The nation's death rate has

Herding is a responsibility for many young Bolivians. However, it prevents some from getting much schooling.   United Nations Photo 148032/Jean Pierre Laffont

dropped and life expectancy has increased in recent decades. Yet its infant mortality rate remains extremely high. A baby born in Bolivia is twelve times more likely to die in its first year than a baby born in the United States. Often births take place at home with midwives instead of doctors attending. This makes complications especially dangerous. Children living in unheated homes at high altitude are particularly vulnerable to throat and lung infections. Complications of poor diet, lack of basic vaccinations, and diarrhea kill many children. Sometimes ignorance is the culprit. Insecticide may be used to kill head lice, causing far more harm than good.

Disease also endangers adults. A lack of sanitation can cause intestinal disorders. Rural beliefs may prevent a person from getting to a doctor. Many Bolivians blend modern medicine with native curing practices in the same way they mix religious beliefs. They may seek doctors if they believe their ailments are natural. But if they believe the causes are supernatural, they may go to native curers or magicians. However, even those who desire modern doctors cannot always find them. Doctors are particularly scarce in rural areas. All too often, coping simply means accepting the inevitable with as little fuss as possible.

Bolivians look for ways to accept their lot. They may find psychological comfort in native and Catholic rituals and doctrines. They may enjoy the break in routine provided by the many annual festivals sponsored in each town and city.

And there is always coca in one form or another. In its mildest form, travelers may sip *mate de coca* to relieve a touch of *sorojche*. More often, laborers turn to the raw coca leaves they carry in waist pouches as their ancestors have been doing for centuries. They believe that chewing the dry, grayish-green leaves hour after hour will strengthen their endurance—or at least ease their suffering.

This is not to say that the situation is hopeless—far from it. For the most part, Bolivians today are far better off than their grandparents. But while progress is measured in generations, every Bolivian must live hour by hour. For most in the 1990's, many of the hours remain hard indeed.

A market woman in La Paz offers traditional remedies. These may be used if an illness is attributed to a supernatural cause.   Hutchison Library/John Hatt

Running the Nation

In 1985 Bolivia's economy became so troubled that President Hernán Siles Zuazo realized he would not be able to finish his term. Three years earlier he had become the first constitutional president of a new civilian era, but his political triumph did not cure deep economic troubles. The government's huge, poorly paid work force demanded raises. Siles Zuazo gave in, but that worsened severe inflation. New demands came from workers and countless other Bolivians.

Few people could afford to buy foreign goods, so the government lost income from import duties. Tin production was barely more than half what it had been eight years earlier, so the government lost money from mineral exports. These were the things the government depended on the most for its money. Taxes didn't help much, because the unfair system let off those most able to pay. A huge debt that the government owned to foreign banks made difficult times even worse.

The constitution entitled a president to a four-year term, but Siles Zuazo decided to hold a new election a year early. Why risk a coup and a new military dictatorship?

Two Capitals?

Reference books invariably list two capitals for Bolivia. Some call Sucre the judicial capital and La Paz the administrative capital. Others call Sucre the official capital and La Paz the de facto capital. Bolivians themselves say Sucre is their capital. But just when the question seems to be settled, they add that La Paz is their seat of government. Don't "capital" and "seat of government" mean the same thing?

Not in twentieth-century Bolivia.

In Spanish times there was no confusion. Sucre (then called Chuquisaca) ruled as the colonial capital of Upper Peru. With independence the city became a national capital, taking the name Sucre in 1840.

In the 1890's, political parties with little support in Sucre (but plenty in La Paz) won control of the national government. Before long most government offices moved. Today only the Supreme Court remains in Sucre. The president and congress govern from La Paz. Foreign nations build their embassies there. In short, La Paz looks and functions like a national capital. Yet the change has never been formalized.

Sucre remains the capital of Bolivia.

Bolivia's Supreme Court Building in Sucre.   Embassy of Bolivia

A Government of Law—and Tradition

When problems are severe in Bolivia, replacing an ineffective president may seem more important than precisely following an election schedule. The country does have a modern constitution. Yet tradition places great faith in one strong, central leader. Bolivians look to both in coping with the severe problems they face.

The Bolivian government has three branches. The chief officer of the executive branch is the president, who both heads the government and leads the nation. (Many countries, especially those outside the Americas, divide these functions. A monarch or president is leader of the

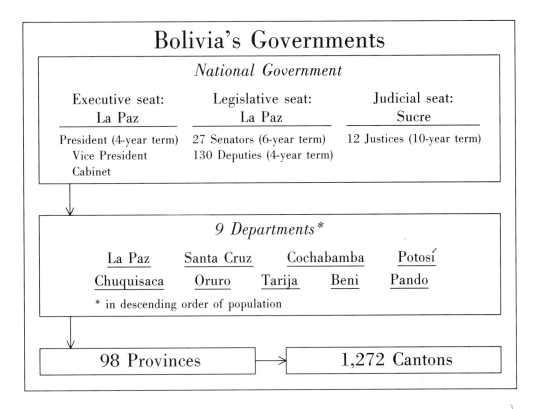

Bolivia's Governments

National Government

Executive seat: La Paz	Legislative seat: La Paz	Judicial seat: Sucre
President (4-year term) Vice President Cabinet	27 Senators (6-year term) 130 Deputies (4-year term)	12 Justices (10-year term)

9 Departments*

La Paz	Santa Cruz	Cochabamba	Potosí
Chuquisaca	Oruro	Tarija	Beni	Pando

* in descending order of population

98 Provinces	→	1,272 Cantons

nation, but a prime minister or party chairman leads the government and has the real power.) The president is elected by a majority of the popular vote. If no candidate gets a majority, the legislature then picks the president. This usually happens. The legislature chose the last three presidents—in 1982, 1985, and 1989.

The legislative branch, or congress, consists of a Senate and a Chamber of Deputies. The senators and deputies are also elected by direct popular vote. Adult Bolivians have the right to vote for senators, deputies, and the president. The final branch of government, the Supreme Court, consists of justices elected by a majority vote of both houses of the legislature.

Though some details are different, this structure resembles the

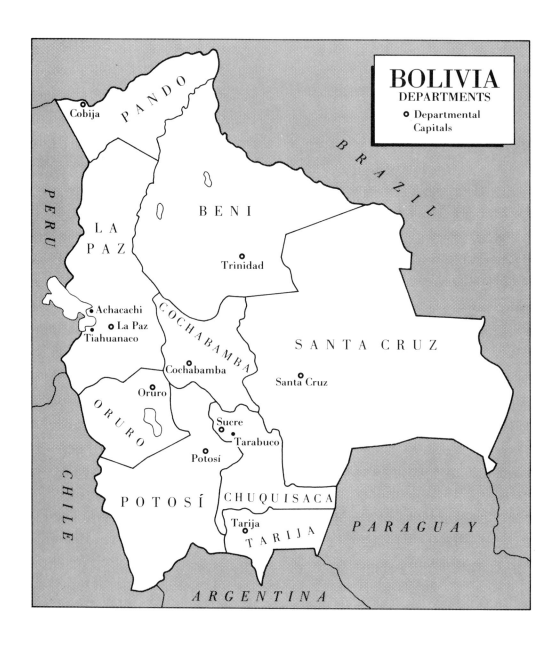

BOLIVIA
DEPARTMENTS
- o Departmental Capitals

PANDO

Cobija

PERU

LA PAZ

BENI

Trinidad

BRAZIL

Achacachi
La Paz
Tiahuanaco

COCHABAMBA

SANTA CRUZ

Cochabamba

Santa Cruz

ORURO

Oruro

Sucre
Tarabuco

Potosí

POTOSÍ

CHUQUISACA

PARAGUAY

Tarija

TARIJA

CHILE

ARGENTINA

United States system of government in its basic form. Both employ branches to create a *separation of powers.* The hope is that each branch will be accountable to the others, thus preventing too much power in any one place. Nonetheless, in practice the Bolivian system is very different from that in the United States. The president usually dominates the government. Presidential programs usually pass without much resistance from the legislature or the court.

The relationship between Bolivia's national government and its regional governments demonstrates just how influential the president is. Bolivia is divided into nine departments. Each has its own capital city and a government led by a prefect. The departments, in turn, are divided into provinces that are led by subprefects. But these regional officials are not elected by the people. The prefects and subprefects are all appointed by the president. So are the mayors of all the departmental capitals. In short, the president chooses the leaders of all Bolivia's regions and major cities. Even the cantons, subdivisions of the provinces, are under indirect presidential control. Their leaders, called *corregidores*, are chosen by the prefects, appointees of the president.

Nonetheless, the national government is not in complete control of local affairs. Municipal councils are elected by the people. And in rural areas, there are governing syndicates completely independent of the national government. These replaced rural *patróns*, who before the 1952 revolution ruled their *haciendas* without much interference from authorities. The government is now much more involved in rural affairs, but the syndicates do operate as local governments to a limited degree. For example, they investigate minor crimes and impose punishments. A syndicate shares power among twelve officers. However, its secretary-general usually dominates—just as the president does at the national level.

The strength of the president (and the rural secretaries-general) comes from the fact that Bolivians traditionally associate authority with a person. Spain's monarchs (for as long as they ruled American colonies) held absolute power. They laughed at British monarchs who shared power with a Parliament and accepted accountability to the law. A Spanish king was the law! Even today, the Roman Catholic Church gives Bolivians an important example of supreme individual authority. There is no procedure for church members, priests, or even cardinals to overrule the pope.

While the power of the Bolivian president is great, it is hardly absolute—as Siles Zuazo learned. Outside the formal government, three groups in particular have important influence in national affairs. The first is the military, which has repeatedly taken control of the government. For that reason, a Bolivian president must carefully consider military interests before taking any major action.

The second group is organized labor. Strikes by miners, teachers, or other government workers, and especially general strikes, can disrupt

Marchers in La Paz, organized by labor unions, protest 1986 tax increases. AP/Wide World Photos

the economy and put severe pressure on the government. The Bolivian Workers Central, a national labor federation, was established by the revolutionary government in 1952. From then until the late 1980's its leader Juan Lechín was one of the most important men in Bolivia.

Bolivia's political parties form the last group. More than a dozen usually participate in an election, but recently about three quarters of Bolivia's voters have supported one of three parties. The oldest is the MNR, now led by Gonzalo Sánchez de Lozada. Around 1970 some former MNR leaders quit and helped form the Revolutionary Movement of the Left. Its leader, Jaime Paz Zamora, became Bolivia's president in August 1989. The third important party is Nationalist Democratic Action, led by former dictator Hugo Banzer. Because no recent presidential candidate has received a majority of the popular votes, parties worked together to form governments. After the 1989 election, congressmen from Banzer's party supported Paz Zamora when the legislature chose him as president. In turn, Paz Zamora agreed to accept a vice president and several cabinet members from Banzer's party.

The Economy and the Government's Role

Just as the president dominates the nation's system of government, the government dominates the national economy. Again, Spanish tradition accounts for this feature of Bolivian national life. In colonial times, the Spanish king owned all the mineral wealth of his American colonies. A miner needed royal permission to work and had to give one fifth of his production to the king. When Spanish colonies won independence, they adopted this principle. Mineral wealth became the property of the nations, not of individual landowners. Today, the same principle applies to oil and natural gas.

Bolivia's Economy in Brief

Gross Domestic Product (GDP) is the total value of the final goods and services produced in a nation in all the ways listed below. The per capita GDP shows, on average, the value of final goods and services produced by each person.

Growth figures show that the 1960's and 1970's were relatively prosperous decades, whereas severe hardship followed in the 1980's. Times were especially hard from 1982 to 1986.

Principal Indicators:

GDP	$4.85 billion (1987)
GDP average annual growth	4.7% (1960–80)
	–1.6% (1980–87)
Per capita GDP	$721 (1987)
Per capita GDP average annual growth	2.2% (1960–80)
	–4.3% (1980–87)

Economic Activity	*% of GDP* (1987)	*Average annual growth* (1960–80)	(1980–87)
Agriculture	23.3	3.6%	1.8%
Financial services	14.2	6.3%	–2.5%
Government	13.7	7.3%	2.2%
Commerce	12.6	5.8%	0.6%
Manufacturing	10.8	6.3%	–5.8%
Mining	10.1	3.1%	–7.8%
Transportation and communication	7.3	6.8%	1.3%
Construction	2.9	5.6%	–5.0%
Electricity, gas, and water	0.9	7.2%	2.6%

Mineral wealth is crucial to Bolivia. Mining has always been a major industry, and oil and natural-gas production have become an important source of income. The government not only claims all this subsoil wealth, it owns the companies that mine and process much of it. Probably none is as important as the Bolivian Mining Corporation, formed in 1952 when the government seized control of the three largest tin-mining companies. Small- and medium-size mining companies remain privately owned, but the national company produces most of the nation's tin. The Bolivian government also owns companies related to mining. Its National Railroad Corporation provides a means to transport ore, and its National Smelting Corporation processes tin, silver, antimony, and lead.

The government is less involved in economic activities unrelated to its subsoil resources. Nonetheless, it owns the National Electricity Corporation and part of Lloyd Aéreo Boliviano, the country's major airline. It controls sugar production, and is thus involved in the country's food-processing industry.

The makeup of Bolivia's economy has changed over the last couple of generations, particularly since the 1952 revolution. Mining forms a much smaller portion of the economy than it once did. Even so, the country exports not only tin but zinc, antimony, lead, copper, tungsten, gold, and silver. Mining still accounts for two thirds of the nation's exports. For that reason, it remains crucial.

The manufacturing portion of the economy has overtaken mining. This is partly because oil and natural-gas production is included in this sector. However, Bolivia also processes wood, food, and beverages and manufactures equipment, machinery, and metal and wood products. Manufacturing contributed a lot to the enormous increase in the country's commercial activities in the 1960's and 1970's.

Agriculture is the largest sector of the economy. The region most important to the nation's wealth is around Santa Cruz and in a zone to the northwest of the city. Here farmers grow cotton, sugarcane, corn, and rice. Ranchers raise beef and poultry. In the montaña to the west, production includes sugar, coffee, tobacco, potatoes, grains, and citrus and other fruits. Even so, only about 3 percent of Bolivia's land is farmed, partly because so much is unsuitable for any crop. Some potentially good land remains unused because it is far from populated areas. Of the land that is used much consists of poor soil in the harsh climate of the altiplano. There, many Bolivian herders and farmers produce just enough to keep themselves and their families alive. Their potatoes, grains, and beans; their chickens, pigs, and goats; their herds of sheep and llama are not headed for national or international markets. They do not help feed city people, and Bolivia must sometimes import food. These crops do not earn foreign dollars that could help everyone in the country.

Coca production has become a special case in recent years. Coca is still grown for traditional purposes—brewing *mate de coca* and chewing. But planting in the montaña has increased dramatically to supply leaves used in the illegal manufacture of cocaine. Bolivian cocaine is worth billions of dollars a year to traffickers. This money certainly helps the Bolivian economy. In the late 1980's it brought in more money than all the country's legal exports combined. Even so, cocaine may be less beneficial to the economy than it seems. Traffickers pay no taxes on cocaine, and they invest most of their earnings outside the country. Furthermore, cocaine may turn out to be profitable only for a short time.

Coping as a Nation

Bolivia as a nation faces severe hardships that make it the second poorest nation in South America (after Guyana). Its leaders are often left with difficult choices and must cope as best they can. Economic and political problems are so closely related that they aggravate each other, as the crisis of 1985 again proved. Numerous long-term or recurring problems have made it difficult to improve the situation. These are the most serious:

Military Rule and Repression

Periods of military dictatorships have plagued Bolivia throughout its history. In the twentieth century, dictators seized power in the thirties, forties, and early fifties. Still another era of military rule began in 1964, and civilian rule was not firmly reestablished until 1982. Presidents have been overthrown because they are *expected* to be such strong leaders. When things go wrong, a president seems weak, and a coup may follow. The new military leader typically argues that constitutional government is an admirable goal for the future, but that a crisis has made it impossible in the short term. The fact that coups have succeeded so often encourages new military leaders, and a military dictator is as likely as an elected civilian to be overthrown by a coup.

Repression often accompanies military rule. Dictators have used deadly force against striking miners and have arrested numerous opposition leaders. This occurred throughout the latest era of military rule. In 1980 the leader of a political party died during a coup. Civilian presidents can also be severe. During part of 1986, Víctor Paz Estenssoro refused to allow peaceful protests or political and union meetings. Some mine union leaders were held without trial.

Unstable Government

Four Bolivians ruled for thirty-one years of the thirty-seven years from 1952 to 1989: Víctor Paz Estenssoro, Hernán Siles Zuazo, René Barrientos, and Hugo Banzer. None served fewer than three years at a stretch, which suggests fairly stable government. Nonetheless, Bolivia has experienced briefer periods of political chaos. Three dictators with widely varying policies ruled in the two years following the death of Barrientos in 1969. Each was overthrown. An even more confused period followed Banzer's overthrow in 1978. Dictators and temporary civilian presidents appointed by the legislature followed one after another. One election was indecisive, another was called off, and public protests became violent at times. The uncertainty lasted four years until Siles Zuazo's election in 1982. Such struggles preoccupy the government for years at a time—taking attention away from national issues.

Corruption
Bolivians frequently use official positions to pursue their own interests. For example, people in authority may give jobs or contracts to their own relatives. Most believe they are fulfilling traditional family obligations and do not consider these acts as corrupt. Nonetheless, such acts prevent competition, which in turn can lead to greater expenses or poorer results when work is done.

The problem involves far more than family loyalties. Corruption happens all over the world, but Bolivia is especially vulnerable because of its weak economy. The government cannot pay its workers adequately, so many feel they must increase their incomes. They use their positions to earn bribes. This type of corruption is so common, in business as well as government, that many Bolivians consider it inevitable or business-as-usual. Most seriously, police and even high government officials often take bribes to allow illegal activity. The worst case in recent years involved Luis García Meza, a military dictator who protected cocaine traffickers operating in the country.

An Inefficient Workforce
This problem is most visible in Bolivian agriculture where so many farmers and herders produce so

President Lydia Gueiler Tejada appears with her chief of staff, General Luis García Meza, in 1980. A few weeks later he seized power in a coup. AP/Wide World Photos

little. The government's control of so much of the nation's business has also led to inefficiency because efficiency is not the government's only concern. It also wants to keep as many people working as possible. As a result, however, its mining company at one point employed three office workers for every person working in the mines. Of course, corruption in both government and private business further reduce the amount of wealth produced in the nation.

The problem, however, goes much deeper. Bolivians stop work for various reasons—often to strike for better working conditions or to attend one of the many annual festivals. Old attitudes and practices also affect enough workers to have a serious impact on production. Spaniards who colonized South America considered manual labor beneath their dignity. Some of their descendants feel the same way. Rural farmers, on the other hand, may not know new methods or be able to afford them. Or they may be afraid to try them. Without crops they

Animals draw plows across an altiplano field as they have for centuries. Agriculture in the region has not been modernized.   Hutchison Library/Brian Moser

would go hungry, maybe starve. Should they risk what little they have on something unfamiliar?

Overdependence on Mining

An economy centered around mining has caused booms and busts because the world's demand for minerals varies a great deal. Also, Bolivia's tin ore is low-grade and located high in the Andes. High refining and transportation costs make Bolivian tin more expensive than tin from Asian suppliers. When world demand for tin falls, Bolivia is the first exporter to be hurt. This has been a constant problem since colonial times. For decades, the country's leaders have tried to develop other industries, and they have made definite progress. But minerals are still the best legal source of foreign exchange, and that means mining will continue to be important to Bolivia's economy.

All these problems are complicated by the fact that they aggravate one another. For example, a period of political chaos is likely to frighten off investors who might have helped form new businesses and create new jobs. Unemployment will then stay high and people will go without goods or services they might otherwise have had. These poor conditions might lead to an economic crisis, another political crisis, and continued unstable government. A similar cycle occurs when the weak economy leaves teachers desperate for a better standard of living. They strike so often that many students don't get the education needed to become skilled workers. That problem perpetuates an inefficient work force and a weak economy.

In short, Bolivian leaders must face all the nation's long-term problems at once; they are too closely related to handle one by one. At the same time, ordinary Bolivians must be allowed the means to survive from one day to the next. The task of Bolivia's leaders is immense.

A New Round

In 1985 Víctor Paz Estenssoro, Bolivia's revolutionary leader of the 1950's and 1960's, returned to the presidency. He took immediate steps to end the extreme inflation that had brought down his predecessor. He won approval for higher, fairer taxes for wealthy Bolivians. He increased the efficiency of the government and companies it controls. He ended government subsidies. His success in ending the inflation astounded many Bolivians and foreigners alike.

There is, however, another way to describe what he did: He laid off thousands of mine workers, and unemployment rose dramatically. He stopped giving ordinary Bolivians money they had counted on to help pay for food, medicine, and transportation. Naturally protests followed, especially from organized labor. Paz Estenssoro answered in 1986 by suspending rights and arresting labor leaders.

In the short term, Paz Estenssoro ended a dangerous economic crisis. But in doing so he lowered the living standards of many Bolivians. Some problems were eased, others aggravated. Bolivia may have made long-term progress, but its most basic problems remain. No quick, simple program will solve them.

A Place
on the Planet

For every Bolivian alive today there are seven hundred people elsewhere in the world. The great majority live in much larger and more
influential nations. Bolivia nonetheless affects its neighbors and its
world in important ways. For example, South American leaders have
often pointed out that Bolivia makes war on the continent less likely.
Located at South America's center, it reduces the borders and potential
trouble spots between large neighbors. It completely separates Peru and
Argentina, rivals from colonial times.

  South Americans have a saying: "If Bolivia did not exist, it would
be necessary to create it."

Common Bonds

Sometimes Bolivia seems friendless. Since it lost its Pacific coast in 1879, it has tried to recover an outlet to the sea. Early in this century, Chile signed a treaty allowing Bolivia to use Arica and Antofagasta as free ports. Yet the cities remained Chilean. In recent decades Bolivia has sought United Nations help in acquiring a Pacific outlet. Nonetheless it remains landlocked.

At other times Bolivia is very much a part of a community of Latin American nations. As past members of the Spanish empire, Bolivia and most of its neighbors share a common language and history. They also share problems. Most Latin American nations have struggled with slow development and dictatorships. Bolivia's move away from dictatorship reflects a trend on the continent for the 1980's. Also, Latin American nations worry together about being misunderstood by the United States. They point out that international press coverage of their affairs is scant. They share foreign-policy problems. Some of the most serious—drug trafficking, debt, and environmental dangers—are discussed below.

Another common problem is the threat from violent guerrilla bands that want to incite revolutions. Rural Bolivians, who have already won land and status in their own revolution, rarely back guerrillas. Still, bands have entered the country trying to win support or set up bases. Argentine-born Ché Guevara, who helped Fidel Castro to bring a revolutionary government to Cuba, came in during the 1960's, only to be killed by the Bolivian army. More recently, the Shining Path guerrilla group of Peru sent at least a few people into Bolivia. The government blamed them for the murder of a Peruvian in La Paz in 1988.

On the widest scale, Bolivia is a member of the Organization of American States and the United Nations. It has relations with communist as well as capitalist countries. The Soviet Union helped Bolivia establish and operate an astronomical observatory in Tarija. Cuba and Bolivia have a scientific and technical pact to improve health care. Bolivia's most important relationships, however, are with Western nations and Japan. Most of its trade is with Argentina, the United States, and Brazil. Other important trading partners are Great Britain, West Germany, Japan, Chile, and Peru.

As a poor country, Bolivia has often accepted assistance from outside. Argentina and Brazil helped it develop energy sources and construct railroads. Japan helped with the construction of its international airport in Santa Cruz. The United States has made grants for technical, economic, and military programs. Help has also come from world organizations, including the Inter-American Development Bank, the World Bank, and agencies of the United Nations. Foreign charitable organizations assist individual Bolivians.

Bolivia's natural resources, in turn, are important to the world, particularly the West. The most obvious example is tin, a vital metal in wartime (as well as peacetime) industry. If a major conflict cut off tin from Asia, Bolivia would become the only major supplier to the West. Exactly that happened during World War II.

The circumstances then allowed Bolivia to establish an important precedent. In 1937 Bolivia had formed its own national oil company and seized property belonging to Standard Oil of New Jersey. No Latin American country had ever taken over the property of an American multinational company. Standard Oil wanted its property or compensation. The matter dragged on for years until it became clear how valuable Bolivia's tin would be to the Allies in World War II. Standard Oil finally settled for a token payment. Bolivia had made possible a process of nationalization that other Latin American countries followed.

A Desire for Control

Most of the time, however, Bolivia cannot manage events as it did during the war. As a small country, it worries about being controlled by outsiders. Bolivians see a dangerous, recurring theme in their history: outside powers taking advantage of their smaller country. Their ancestors slaved to enrich Spanish monarchs for three hundred years, but Spain did little to improve its colony. Later Bolivia became a poor nation and an easy target for neighbors that eventually stripped away half its territory. Its minerals continued to enrich foreign nations while the country remained in poverty. There even seemed to be Bolivian accomplices. Simón Patiño became a fabulously wealthy tin entrepreneur and then left to invest his money in Europe. Bolivians see him as an archvillain who helped foreigners sack the nation. Fear of new exploitation is a compelling force in Bolivia's relations with the world today.

Bolivia will not allow the United States to build a permanent military base on its soil as some countries have done. It feels that U.S. plans for a satellite to monitor coca growth violate its rights. A concern about foreign control even affects Bolivia's relations with the Roman Catholic Church. Parish priests protested to the Vatican in 1988 when a Spaniard and an Italian were named auxiliary bishops in Bolivia.

Tension over foreign influence is most visible in economic matters. Bolivians negotiating tin prices with buyers in the United States and Europe usually bring up World War II. Since Bolivia came through then, its negotiators argue, shouldn't it now be guaranteed a good price for its tin and a steady share of the world market? No such guarantee has ever come. There is a particularly strong feeling among miners that they are exploited by foreigners.

Bolivian leaders must frequently deal with foreign governments, international organizations, and banks. When they do, political opponents invariably claim that they are becoming puppets. Foreign control is always a political issue, and it affects how Bolivia's leaders act toward other nations.

The Dilemma of Cocaine

Drug trafficking has become one of Bolivia's most serious foreign-policy issues. People in some of the wealthiest nations in the world demanded more and more cocaine during the 1980's. Never before had the narcotic been used in such quantity. People in the United States, France, Great Britain, Spain, West Germany, and other nations now spend billions of dollars each year for the illegal drug.

For Bolivians the temptation was enormous. The manufacture of cocaine is illegal in Bolivia, but growing coca is not. Tens of thousands of small growers recently planted it for the first time. Bolivians continue producing coca plants for the mild traditional products, *mate de coca* and leaves for chewing. However, about twenty times as much is going toward cocaine production.

Without a doubt, many impoverished laborers have improved their lives by supplying coca for the cocaine trade. Traffickers encourage them with words as well as money. Hadn't Western Europe and the United States benefited from Bolivian tin, at the same time leaving Bolivia in poverty? Small rural growers could easily be convinced that cocaine meant justice—especially during the hard times of the 1980's. Traffickers also made charitable donations to poor individuals and communities to win public support.

A few Bolivians benefit a great deal. Corrupt civil servants and police officers in the right places earned huge bribes by allowing drug operations to take place without interference. Many such officials even paid their superiors thousands of dollars for assignments that put them in a position to collect bribes. Major drug traffickers themselves have become fabulously wealthy. Yet only a fraction of the cocaine profit ever returns to Bolivia. Traffickers spend or invest five times as much overseas—much the way exploitive tin entrepreneurs once did.

For most, the improved standard of living has been slight or brief. In 1984 100 pounds (45 kilograms) of coca leaves could bring $350, but by 1988 the price had dropped to $20. Though coca continued to bring more income than other crops, most of the advantage for individual small growers disappeared. Meanwhile, cocaine is beginning to hurt Bolivians themselves. One of the nation's leading biologists discovered a cocaine factory by chance while studying plants in the lowlands. He, his guide, and his pilot were shot to death. Later, a congressman was killed after he claimed to have information in the case. Worse yet, cocaine addiction among young Bolivians—not just foreigners—has begun to climb.

Bolivia's recent civilian presidents have found themselves in a difficult position. The United States government, desperate to cut off the supply of cocaine to its people, pressured Bolivia to fight drug trafficking. At one point U.S. foreign aid was reduced because Bolivia had not adequately cut back on coca acreage. Yet many Bolivians argued that their country shouldn't have to pay for the solution of a foreign problem. Members of the Bolivian congress, for example, correctly pointed out that users in the United States and other countries finance the cocaine trade.

The government of the late 1980's did move against drug running. It allowed a United Nations agency to help coca growers switch to other crops. Bolivia also worked with the United States. In 1986 President Víctor Paz Estenssoro allowed U.S. troops and drug enforcement agents to enter the country in a joint operation against traffickers. He faced immediate protests from those who said he was putting foreign interests ahead of Bolivian interests. Paz Estenssoro nonetheless allowed the drug-enforcement agents to stay, even after the troops had finished their operation. In 1989 his successor, Jaime Paz Zamora, announced he would continue efforts to fight drug trafficking. But Bolivia puts limits on what it will allow the United States to do. Paz Estenssoro would not permit the aerial spraying of herbicides to destroy coca crops. Paz Zamora said he will act only in ways that protect the rights and well-being of Bolivians.

The effort has had limited success in the short run. The 1986 operation reduced the supply of cocaine, if only for a short time. And in 1988 Bolivian police arrested Roberto Suárez, reputed to be the nation's most powerful drug trafficker. The long-range effect is less certain, but certainly the world demand for cocaine will be the most important factor. The narcotic's use in the United States will likely fall in coming years. No one can say by how much, however, and the same may not be true

Working in Bolivia, an agent of the U.S. Drug Enforcement Administration prepares to destroy a pit where coca leaves are soaked. Soaking is an early step in the process of refining cocaine. Drug Enforcement Administration

of other consuming nations. Meanwhile, other leaders have already taken over from Suárez, and coca acreage remains many times higher than what is needed for traditional uses.

The Debt Crisis

Another major concern Bolivia faces is foreign debt. The Bolivian government owes billions of dollars to foreign banks and governments. The money was borrowed with the idea that it would help to develop the nation's economy. Leaders hoped a stronger economy would enable them to pay back the loans, but by 1985 it was clear that the strategy had failed.

Again Bolivian leaders found themselves caught between the needs of their own people and their obligations to people abroad. If they refused to pay their loans, Bolivia would find it hard to borrow money in the future. If they paid, they would further reduce the living standards of their own people.

In the midst of its inflation crisis of 1985, Bolivia missed payments on its foreign loans. Why, asked its leaders, should it sacrifice the welfare of its people to accommodate foreign bankers?

Bolivia was able to suspend payment in part because it was not alone. Other Latin American nations had also borrowed far beyond their means. By 1987 Latin American governments owed $415 billion. Bolivia's $4.8-billion debt was a very serious problem for its weak economy, but it amounted to just over 1 percent of that total debt.

It made no sense for the creditors (the banks and governments who had lent the money) to punish Bolivia or try to force it to pay the debt. They feared that Latin American nations would band together and refuse to pay at all if they were too harsh with any one country. Instead, Bolivia and its creditors began a long, complicated process of negotiations to settle the debt. Some creditors agreed to take 11 cents for every dollar owed, for example, but most of the debt is still unresolved.

Conservation

Mineral wealth is not the only Bolivian resource vital to the outside world. The debt crisis had an unexpected and positive side effect. Bolivia made a contribution to the international effort to preserve the Earth's environment.

Conservationists worldwide worry about the destruction of tropical rain forests along the Earth's equatorial belt. These dense forests provide much of the oxygen in the atmosphere and contain millions of species of plants and animals. Some of these species have proven very valuable, but most have not yet been studied. Conservationists fear many never will be. Countries struggling to pay international debts are destroying forests for quick profits from their resources, such as timber. Some are simply being burned to open farm or pasture lands. There is no way to replace an extinct species, and permanent harm to the world's climate is a growing concern.

One of the richest rain forests in the world grows around the Amazon River and its tributaries. Most of the area is in Brazil, but tens of millions of acres fall in the Bolivian lowlands. The land is home to nomadic Indians and endangered species including the jaguar, giant otter, and maned wolf. In 1982 Bolivia created a 334,000-acre (135,000-hectare) reserve in its tropical Beni department. Even so, lands just outside the reserve were threatened by cattle ranching. Had the ranches expanded, the country might have been able to slightly reduce food imports. On the other hand, permanent damage to the rain forests might have resulted.

Bolivia agreed to a solution worked out by Conservation Interna-

tional: It is protecting an additional 3.7 million acres (1.5 million hectares) that surrounded the old reserve. This area alone holds more than five hundred species of birds, thirteen types of endangered plants and animals, and more species of trees than grow in all of North America. Some of the land is being left undisturbed, some is being preserved as a hunting ground for the Indians, and still more will go for carefully managed agricultural and forestry development. In exchange, Bolivia's foreign debt was reduced by $650,000.

Bolivia's mineral wealth has made an important contribution to the world for centuries. Its rain forests, if preserved, can do the same in the future. Bolivia has also shown it can occasionally be a leader in the world. In 1809 it was the first region in South America to declare its independence. It led again in 1937 with its nationalization policy. Its revolution of 1952 provided an important example of land reform. In the late 1980's Brazil, Chile, Costa Rica, and Peru all explored the possibility of protecting land in exchange for reductions in their foreign debts. With its conservation experiment, Bolivia had again showed that a country need not be a superpower, or even a regional power, to make important contributions to the planet.

The Beni River winds through Bolivia's lowlands in part of the ecologically important Amazon basin. Conservation International

The Danger and Promise Ahead

The old Aymara folktales warn of a world full of dangers that can consume the witless at any moment. The severe, chronic problems that have plagued Bolivia since its birth seem to confirm that. Nonetheless, problems that have dogged a society for generations *can* be solved. Bolivia proved that in the 1950's by overthrowing a racist legal system that had exploited its Indians since the sixteenth century. Today its land holds diverse resources. Its people have a variety of traditions from which to draw solutions. These strengths can be used to shape a nation that allows Bolivians to live secure, happy lives in a style of their own choice.

The leaders of the 1952 revolution are too old to take Bolivia into the next century. President Jaime Paz Zamora and his successors will not have the revolutionary reputation that gave so much strength to leaders of Víctor Paz Estenssoro's generation. They will have to prove their leadership in other ways to prevent new bouts of political instability and military dictatorship.

Civilian presidents have ruled the country since 1982, but this development is not necessarily permanent. The country has seen long periods of civilian rule before, only to fall back to military rule. Some dictators have an honored place in Bolivian history; René Barrientos, for example, ruled during a relatively prosperous period in the 1960's. Bolivians who remember him fondly will be alive for many years to come. An economic crisis or a weak civilian leader might again inspire a new dictator to follow him.

At worst, Bolivia's government could fall to another tyrant mainly interested in profits from the cocaine traffic. Narcotics bosses would likely exploit laborers as willingly as any old-style *patrón* or mining lord. The people would earn barely enough to get by, and the nation could spend years as an international outlaw.

At best, Bolivia could enjoy an enduring era of civilian leadership with the opportunity to concentrate on its oldest economic problems. It could use the 1990's to gradually improve living standards in its own way.

Yet even the most successful decade would leave the country with two serious new problems in the twenty-first century. Rapid population growth is the first. A sustained high birth rate would eventually lead to extreme overcrowding and pollution. The resulting tragically high death rate would prevent further growth, but at what cost?

Since Bolivia has more land per person than most countries, this problem seems far off. This is deceiving, however, because the areas

An employee of a La Paz radio station works at a modern video display terminal.
Caroline Penn

with poor soil and a harsh climate can never support a large population. Also, rapid population growth means that a large percentage of Bolivians are children. This in turn causes more immediate problems. How can a poor country provide a decent education for so many?

The government began a family planning program around 1970. However, its policy has been to provide information only about certain methods of birth control, and then only to people who ask for it. Its attention has been on child welfare programs, not plans to reduce population growth.

Environment is the second great problem Bolivia will face in the coming century. The fact that it is already addressing this problem is one of the brightest signs for its future. Nonetheless, Bolivia as a nation must deal with a dilemma like the one that faced some of its miners. They had to decide whether to protect jobs in the short run or insure health in the long run. Bolivia is presented with a temptation to achieve a brief prosperity by cutting or burning through its lowlands for timber or land. Such a policy would be a disaster to the long-term health of the nation and the world.

This is not to say that Bolivia must not use its resources. Its population will remain impoverished if it doesn't. Instead, the country must use them in a way that allows them to replenish themselves. Bolivians could, for example, use wood resources at a modest pace and replace those trees they harvested. The rain forests and all their benefits would live on, and unlimited generations could prosper.

There is no simple model for Bolivians to follow. The countries that developed in the past made serious mistakes (allowing excessive pollution, for example). Bolivia also has a unique geography that must be considered. But here it finds strength. The great difference in altitude might make hydroelectric power ideal for the montaña. Perhaps the harsh sunlight pounding the altiplano will make solar energy especially suitable. The sun has already powered pumps in experiments there. Either source of energy might contribute to a better future without exhausting the land and polluting the air.

Bolivians *do* live in a world as dangerous as the one described in the old tales. They will need all their wits to prosper. But their regions are rich with resources and they have attracted a diverse population. As a land of many parts, Bolivia has much to draw on. There is no law that says its enduring frustrations cannot be conquered and new dangers avoided.

And there is no reason it cannot contribute many things to the world. A Bolivian mathematician has offered a hint about what his country may yet offer. He knew that computers have great difficulty handling human language. He also spoke Aymara, a language unknown to most computer programmers. He found that its orderly structure could be converted into an algebraic code, something a computer could work with easily. Might this help in a program that translates one language to another? He is trying to develop just such a program.

Who can guess what other surprises this unique Hispanic-Indian nation will offer the world?

Suggestions for
Further Reading

Students studying Bolivia can start here to learn more about the topics that interest them the most. All printed works here are in English. However, the Klein and Morner books under "Twentieth-Century History" have detailed bibliographies and include works for students who can read Spanish. An important thing to remember in studying Bolivia is that much information appears in works that are not exclusively devoted to the country.

Bibliography

Geography, Wildlife, and Conservation

Cohn, Jeffrey P. "Elusive Kings of the Wild." *Américas*, July–August 1984, pp. 2–7+.
    A well-illustrated article on South America's big cats.

Oppenheim, Victor. *Exploration: East of the High Andes.* New York: Pageant Press, 1958.
    An explorer's account that includes Bolivia's montaña and lowlands.

Walsh, John. "Bolivia Swaps Debt for Conservation." *Science* 237 (August 7, 1987), pp. 596–97.
  Details of Bolivia's conservation agreement of 1987.

Early History

Arciniegas, Germán, ed. *The Green Continent.* (Translated from Spanish.) New York: Knopf, 1944.
  Contains an account by Bolivian historian Alcides Arguedas that describes the rise of nineteenth-century dictator Mariano Melgarejo.

Arzáns de Orsúa y Vela, Bartolomé. *Tales of Potosí.* Edited by R. C. Padden. (Translated from Spanish.) Providence, RI: Brown University Press, 1975.
  Accounts and legends about colonial Potosí recorded by Arzáns (1676–1736), a lifelong resident.

Fiedel, Stuart J. *Prehistory of the Americas.* Cambridge: Cambridge University Press, 1987.
  An illustrated, up-do-date survey of ancient civilizations in the Americas.

McIntyre, Loren. *The Incredible Inca and Their Timeless Land.* Washington, DC: National Geographic Society, 1975.
  Inca culture and history well illustrated with both drawings and photographs.

Prescott, William H. *History of the Conquest of Peru.* Edited by John Foster Kirk. 2 vols. Philadelphia: J. B. Lippincott Company, 1874.
  A detailed account of the Spanish conquest of the Incas.

Stevens, William K. "Scientists Revive a Lost Secret of Farming." *The New York Times*, November 22, 1988, p. C1.
  Explorations around Lake Titicaca that have led to the rediscovery of farming techniques.

Twentieth-Century History

Klein, Herbert S. *Bolivia: The Evolution of a Multi-Ethnic Society.* New York and Oxford: Oxford University Press, 1982.
  A college-level survey that stresses economics and politics.

Malloy, James M. *Bolivia: The Uncompleted Revolution.* Pittsburgh: University of Pittsburgh Press, 1970.
 A scholarly description of Bolivia's development after the 1952 revolution.

Morner, Magnus. *The Andean Past: Land, Societies, and Conflicts.* New York: Columbia University Press, 1985.
 A survey of Andes civilization from prehistory to the early 1980's. Contains an excellent, up-to-date bibliography.

Zook, David H., Jr. *Conduct of the Chaco War.* New Haven, CT: Bookman Associates, 1960.
 A detailed account of the 1932–35 war between Bolivia and Paraguay.

People and Culture

Barrios de Chungara, Domitila. *Let Me Speak!* With Moema Viezzer. (Translated from Spanish.) New York: Monthly Review Press, 1978.
 Mine life and labor struggles described by a miner's wife.

Bierhorst, John. *The Mythology of South America.* New York: Morrow, 1988.
 Includes sections on Greater Brazil, Gran Chaco, and Central Andes, which cover Bolivia.

Buechler, Hans C., and Judith-Marie Buechler. *The Bolivian Aymara.* New York: Holt, Rinehart and Winston, 1971.
 Family and community life in an Aymara town.

Hickman, Katie. "Bolivia's Crowning Glory." *Américas,* July–August 1987, pp. 22–25+.
 A well-illustrated article for students of all ages on Bolivia's regional hats.

La Barre, Weston. "Aymara Folktales." *International Journal of American Linguistics* 16 (1950), pp. 40–45.
 A difficult scholarly article, but gives brief summaries of Aymara folktales.

Nash, June. *We Eat the Mines and the Mines Eat Us.* New York: Columbia University Press, 1979.
 Life and problems in mining areas; also a good account of the Devil Dance.

Stoddart, Veronica Gould, and A. R. Williams. "Sucre's Colonial Tapestry." *Américas*, January–February 1986, pp. 8–15.
 A well-illustrated description of architecture in Sucre.

Vargas, Manuel. "Oruro: A Parade of Traditions." *Américas*, November–December 1986, pp. 32–35+.
 A well-illustrated description of the Devil Dance.

Williams, A. R. "Music: Rhythms of Daily Life." *Américas*, January–February 1986, pp. 53–55.
 Music and instruments of Bolivia.

Fiction and Poetry

Carpentier, Hortense, and Janet Brof, eds. *Doors and Mirrors: Fiction and Poetry from Spanish America 1920–1970.* (Translated from Spanish.) New York: Grossman Publishers, 1972.
 Includes "The Indian Paulino," a short story by Bolivian writer Ricardo Ocampo.

Colford, William E., ed. *Classic Tales from Spanish America.* (Translated from Spanish.) Great Neck, NY: Barron's, 1962.
 Includes "Indian Justice," a short story by Bolivian writer Ricardo Jaimes Freyre.

Costa du Rels, Adolfo. *Bewitched Lands.* (Translated from Spanish.) New York: Knopf, 1945.
 This novel by a Bolivian writer describes a father-son conflict that represents a changing Bolivia.

Fitts, Dudley, ed. *Anthology of Contemporary Latin American Poetry.* (Translated from Spanish.) Norfolk, CT: New Directions, 1942.
 Includes several works by Bolivian poets Jesús Lara and Raúl Otero Reiche.

Flores, Angel, and Dudley Poole, eds. *Fiesta in November: Stories from Latin America.* (Translated from Spanish.) Boston: Houghton Mifflin, 1942.
 Includes "La Misqui-Simi," a short story by Bolivian writer Adolfo Costa du Rels.

Pausewang, Gudrun. *Bolivian Wedding.* (Translated from German.) New York: Knopf, 1971.
 A clearly written novel that skillfully describes the pride and devotion of rural villagers in the 1930's.

Prada, Renato. *The Breach.* (Translated from Spanish.) Garden City, NY: Doubleday, 1971.

A novel by a modern Bolivian writer about two young men on opposite sides of a rebellion.

Current Events

Daily Report: Latin America. Washington, DC: Government Printing Office.

Includes stories from Bolivian newspapers and broadcast stations translated from Spanish by the Foreign Broadcast Information Service of the United States government.

Latin American Weekly Report. London: Latin American Newsletters, Ltd.

An excellent source of news concerning Bolivia.

New York Times Index. Some large newspapers, including *The New York Times*, have indexes that can be found in reference sections of many libraries. These can be used along with general indexes, such as the *Readers' Guide to Periodical Literature*, to find recent articles on Bolivia.

Filmography and Discography

Few films on Bolivia have been made since the mid-1970's, so those available are dated. One that is still useful and concentrates on health, mining conditions, and poverty is Thames Television's *Bolivia: The Tin Mountain* (1979; 16mm and videocassette, 28 minutes), distributed by the Media Guild, 11722 Sorrento Valley Road, San Diego, CA 92121.

However, Andean music has become popular. Recordings are now widely available in the United States; two sources are Pa'lante, Latin American Record Distributors, P.O. Box 40322, San Francisco, CA 94140, and World Music Institute, 109 West 27th Street, New York, NY 10001.

Bolivia Manta. *Wiñayataqui.* 1984. Stereo CD. 58 minutes. Distributed by World Music Institute, New York. Themes from various regions in Bolivia, Ecuador, and Peru; explanatory booklet includes English notes.

Bolivia. Panpipes. 1987. CD. 46 minutes. Distributed by World Music Institute, New York. On-site recordings from Aymara and Quechua communities made between 1950 and 1973; explanatory booklet includes English notes.

Ernesto Cavour y Su Conjunto. Stereo cassette. 47 minutes. Distributed by Pa'lante Records, San Francisco. Carnival songs and other Bolivian themes in arrangements that emphasize *charango* playing; lyrics in Spanish.

Grupo Aymara. *Pachamama Project.* 1988. Stereo cassette. 41 minutes. Distributed by World Music Institute, New York. Traditional arrangements using Andean instruments; explanatory booklet in English.

Huara. Stereo cassette. 38 minutes. Distributed by Pa'lante Records, San Francisco. Refined, modern arrangements using Andean instruments.

Pukaj Wayra. *Music from Bolivia.* 1981. Stereo LP. 40 minutes. Distributed by World Music Institute, New York. The diablada and other folk music; mostly Spanish and some Quechua lyrics.

Torres, Osvaldo. *Cuentos del Altiplano.* Stereo cassette. 34 minutes. Distributed by Pa'lante Records, San Francisco. Four colorful folk stories of the altiplano told in Spanish.

Index

Numbers in *italics* refer to illustrations. People using multiple Spanish surnames are usually alphabetized by the first surname. For example, Jaime Paz Zamora is listed as Paz Zamora, Jaime.

families, 115, 116, 150–52
   See also women
family planning, 192
Father's Day, 105
Fellman Valarde, José, 122
fer-de-lance, 22
Ferdinand VII, King of Spain, 59, 61
festivals, 2, 116, 125, *126, 127,* 160
flooding, 12, 20, 24, 87
folk art. *See* music; festivals
folktales, 124, 190
Four Corners of the World, 38
France, 56, 183
Francovich, Guillermo, 124
frost, 11, 13, 16

García Meza, Luis, 77, 174, *175*
Gateway to the Sun, *32,* 34–35
German language, 91
Germany, 71
God (Christian), 108, 111, 114
Good Friday, 105
Government Palace, 120
Gran Colombia, 61, *62*
Great Britain, 56, 70, 71, 168, 181, 183
Great Depression, 59, 71
gross domestic product (GDP), 170
Guadelupe, Virgin of, 110, *110,* 117
Guaranian language group, 91
Guatemala, 96–98
Gueiler Tejada, Lydia, 77, 141, *175*
guerrillas, 180
Guevara, Ché, 180
guitar, 127
Guyana, 172

haciendas, 51, 70, 76–79, 81, 83, 85, 167
hail, 11, 114
health care, 76, 115, 158–60, 181
   folk medicine, 160, *161*
herding, 11, 12–13, 27, 53, 132, *159,*
   172, 174–75

Holy Cross festival, 107
housing, 79, 129, 131–32, *130, 131,*
   137–40
Huayna Capac, 34, 38

Illimani, 7, 8–10, *10*
immigrants and immigration, 91, 98
Incas, 2, 33–38, 40, 41–44
   artifacts, *36,* 46, *47*
   conquest of the Aymara, 33–34, 40
   · empire, *25,* 34–38, 92, 104–05
independence, 59, 63, 117
   See also Wars of Independence
Indians, 42–43, 44–46, 49–55, 65, 67, 70,
   75–81, 83–84, 91, 96–98, 100–02,
   147, 150, 150–52
   cultural influence, 118, *119,* 122, 124,
   125–26, 127–28, 194
   national Indian congress, 81
   nomadic, 20, 187, 189
   rebellions, 34, 40, 44, 51–52,
   56
   See also individual cultures;
   campesinas(nos); religion, Indian
"indiobrutos," 76
indios, 76, 83
infant mortality, xiii, 76, 85, 159
inflation, 87, *88,* 152–53, 162, 177–78,
   186
Inter-American Development Bank,
   181
irrigation, 27
Isabella, Queen of Spain, 39
Italian language, 91

jaguars, 17, 24, 187
Jaimes Freyre, Ricardo, 80, 122
Japan, 181
Japanese language, 91
Jesuits, 52–53, 55, 56
Jesus, 105, 110, 114
Juão II, King of Portugal, 39

ABOUT THE AUTHOR

David Nelson Blair belongs to an extended family spread
throughout the Americas. As a child he lived in Bolivia,
and he has recently returned there to visit major cities
and isolated towns. He has a master's degree in Latin
American history, and works as a free-lance editor and
writer.

Blair, David Nelson

The Land and People of
Bolivia